Good Old Somersets

Good Old Somersets

The 1st Battalion Somerset Light Infantry
August–December 1914

Compiled by

Brian Gillard

From contemporary diaries and reports

Matador
9 De Montfort Mews
Leicester LE1 7FW, UK
Tel: (+44) 116 255 9311 / 9312
Email: books@troubador.co.uk
Web: www.troubador.co.uk/matador

ISBN 1 904744 31 1

Typeset in 10pt Hoefler by Troubador Publishing Ltd, Leicester, UK

Matador is an imprint of Troubador Publishing

Printed by The Cromwell Press, Trowbridge, Wiltshire.

To the memory of Corporal Hubert Bonning, a regular soldier, who gave his life for his comrades on 19th December 1914 whilst serving with the Somerset Light Infantry in Flanders.

Relief party going up to the Front Line along Regent Street, Ploegsteert Wood (*Sphere Magazine*)

Contents

Introduction

'Good Old Somersets' was the compliment paid to the 1st Battalion, Somerset Light Infantry by the Brigade Commander, following the action at Le Gheer in October 1914.

The following pages tell the story, of the Battalion from the outbreak of the First World War on 4th August 1914 to the end of the year. The accounts are taken from diaries and recollections of men who served during the first months of the war. They cover the Retreat from Mons, the subsequent Counter-attack on the Aisne and the move to Ypres Salient and ends with the Christmas Truce of 1914.

I was at first going to write a history of the Battalion, but on starting my research, I soon realised I would only be retelling the words of the men who fought at that time. I found that their accounts brought alive more graphically the trials, hardships, and indeed, humour of the British Infantryman than I ever could.

The following chronicles are almost entirely as written in 1914. I have only made the occasional alteration to the text to clarify or improve the context of the reports. I have also adapted some descriptions of actions from the *History of the Somerset Light Infantry* published in 1921, to give perspective to the battles in which the Battalion participated.

The main story is told from the official War Diaries (WO 95/1499) held at the National Archive, Kew. These have been transcribed, and are the first item for each day. There then follows personal accounts of the day taken from diaries and newspaper reports by men serving in the Battalion. The main sources are:

- Extracts from diaries and correspondence of Officers and Men written at the time.
- Orders and Messages relating to the Battalion contained in the War Diary of the 11th Infantry Brigade (WO 95/1486-89)
- Articles from local newspapers published in 1914
- Other items held at the National Archive including maps, medal rolls, court martial proceedings and war diaries of other units.
- Papers and documents held in the Somerset Light Infantry Archive, Taunton (By kind permission of the Trustees)

- Extracts from books containing references to men serving with the Somersets in 1914.
- Documents held by in the Liddle Collection in the library of the University of Leeds
- Maps from the Imperial War Museum/Naval and Military Press CD-Roms of the Official History and Trench Map Archive

Details of the sources are shown in Appendix 1.

I have thought it best to enter events taken from personal diaries against the dates on which they were recorded which were not always identical to those in the War Diary. At this time of so much action and movement, diaries may only have been written up several days later. Recollections may have been confused and accordingly dates and timing very approximate. Overnight operations have also resulted in some events being recorded over two or more days.

Wherever possible, approval has been obtained to reproduce the material. If I have inadvertently used any copyright articles, I must express my apologies. After such a long passage of time, it has proved impossible to trace the actual sources of much of the work used.

This is not a history, as it does not – unless needed to set the context – deal with the national events relating to the outbreak and first months of The Great War. Nor are there details of the military strategy and movements of the British Expeditionary Force. This book is limited to the experiences of one infantry battalion, amongst the sixty or so, who went to France in August 1914.

Brian Gillard
May 2004

Acknowledgements

The origins of this book lie with a recollection of my wife's mother, Daisy Rowland, and my thanks go to her for giving me an interest that has taken up far too much of my time over the past few years.

Daisy was born in 1915, and some time ago she reminisced about a soldier's Glengarry cap that had hung over the family's fireplace when she was a little girl in a Devon village. The children were told that it had belonged to Uncle Hubert who had died in the War, but nothing more was ever added.

She said she had always wondered about Uncle Hubert, and how he met his death, was there something about it that the family did not want to discuss? At that time I was researching my father's record in the 2/4th Somersets, where he won the Military Medal, so had some idea of how to trace a service record. I therefore checked his death on the Commonwealth War Graves Commission website. There I found that Corporal Hubert Bonning had been killed in action on 19th December 1914 whilst serving with the Somerset Light Infantry, and was buried at The Strand Cemetery, Ploegsteert Belgium. I then looked up the War Diary and found details of the attack on the 'Birdcage' on that day when many Somersets were lost. From his Regimental Number, I realised that he would have been a regular soldier, and that he had probably enlisted about 1900.

Hubert's service record must have been amongst those destroyed in the Blitz in 1940 and so I was unable to find out any more about him. Then I came across a booklet published by Jim Glibberly on the Broadway and Horton war memorial. These villages are near Ilminster where Hubert Bonning's family lived. Thanks to his help, I found that there was a Memorial Book in Ilminster Parish Church, and from this I confirmed that Hubert was a Regular, and the book added that he was killed bringing back a wounded man to the trenches. This information was of great comfort to my mother in law, but for a time that was as far as I could go.

On a later visit to the Public Record Office, I came across a book *A Walk around Plugstreet* by Tony Spangoly and Ted Smith, and bought it out of interest. Much of this book covers the actions in and around Ploegsteert Wood in 1914, in which the Somersets played a large part. This aroused my interest in the opening stages of the War, and led me to do further research into the Battalion from mobilisation in

August 1914. For this I must thank the authors, especially Tony, who has encouraged me to set my researches down. With Tony and the War Research Group I have visited many of the places mentioned.

My next breakthrough was on surfing the Web and finding reference to the Liddle Collection of documents at the University of Leeds Library. From the on-line catalogue I saw that they held copies of diaries of Captain Bradshaw and Private Packe. Richard Davies kindly sent me copies of the relevant documents, and to my surprise on opening the envelope the first thing I saw was a photograph of Hubert Bonning and Edward Packe. It appears that Edward, a student at Oxford in August 1914, decided to enlist in the Army. Instead of going to a recruiting office, he presented himself at the nearest barracks in Colchester. Here he was accepted straight into the ranks of the Somerset Light Infantry. It is my supposition that as a raw recruit with no training or experience, an old soldier, Hubert Bonning, became his mentor and friend. A note attached to the photograph speaks of Hubert as "one of those men who can always joke and laugh, no matter how adverse conditions are, from the elements, physical exhaustion, hunger, thirst or danger". When I approached Richard for a better copy of the photograph, he put me in touch with Robin Diblee, Edward's grandson. I must thank Robin and his parents, John and Celia Diblee, for supplying me with copies of the photograph, and for their kind remarks. Thanks also are due to the University Library for allowing me to use extracts from Edward's diaries and correspondence.

My research then led me to the Somerset Light Infantry Archive, at that time held at the Light Infantry Office Taunton. I would like to thank Colonel David Elliot and his staff for allowing me to search for and copy many of the diaries, documents and photographs relevant to the Somersets at this time. I would also express my appreciation to the Trustees of the Archive for allowing me to use the material in the production of this book. I would add that the archive has now been transferred to the Somerset County Record Office, where it has been catalogued and is available to researchers.

I am grateful to the staff of the many archives, newspaper offices and libraries who have assisted me with my research. Also to fellow members of the Somerset Branch of the Western Front Association, who have been able to help me with general queries and with information on Somerset men serving at that time.

In the production of the book, my thanks to Tony Chown for reading the proofs and making many helpful comments, and to Jeremy and Jane of Troubador Publishing Ltd for their help and advice on the publication process.

Finally, I must not forget my family. Thanks to my daughters for ferrying me back and forward to the National Archive, and to Anne for allowing me to neglect her for long periods, whilst visiting battlefields, museums and archives – and particularly for the time spent on the computer at home.

Chapter One

Mobilisation and Embarkation 29th July–23rd August

The 1st Battalion, Prince Albert's Somerset Light Infantry were stationed at Goojerat Barracks, Colchester under the command of Lieutenant Colonel E. H. Swayne. Together with the 1st Battalions, The Rifle Brigade, Hampshire and East Lancashire Regiments they formed the 11th Infantry Brigade of the 4th Division.

The peacetime establishment of the Battalion was approximately 650–700 men. They were all regular soldiers and many had served with the Regiment in The Boer War, on the Northwest Frontier of India or with the 2nd Battalion in Tiensten, China. As well as from the County, many men were recruited from the London and South Wales areas

29th July

Precautionary Mobilisation ordered. Advance Party to Felixstowe. Felixstowe detachment off at 8.30 p.m. to guard ferries, dig trenches, put up wire and loophole houses. All wagons and limbers packed and horses from the town fitted with harness and allowed to return but to be ready for instant requisition, in case of German raid, which was expected. Battalion had to be entrained complete in 2 hours. Everybody confined to barracks. Kits packed and orderlies sleeping on the telephone.

Fresh orders continually coming in. German raids expected. General Mobilisation daily expected and as much as possible done in preparation. (*O. Philby*)

4th August

Orders to mobilise received at 5.00 pm.

1

On Mobilisation the regular troops were joined by reservists to bring the strength of an Active Service Battalion of nearly 1000. The reservists were mainly men who had served with the 'Colours' for a period of years and had returned to civilian life, but were liable to recall in case of emergency and mobilisation. There were also a small proportion of Special Reservists, civilians who trained with the regulars and received a retainer to be called up, if required.

Caillard and Kennedy to Depot with Colours. Clothing fitted. Civilian horses taken in, shod and fitted. Rifles and bayonets overhauled and bayonets and swords sharpened.
(*O Philby*)

Our Brigade Commander was General Hunter-Weston, "Hunter Bunter" the boys called him – one of the finest soldiers and gentlemen you could wish to meet. When we joined his Brigade he told us, "We shall be at war with Germany before I give up this command." and he was plumb right! He must have known more about it than we did. So here is the war and we have got to do something about it.
(*Arthur Cook*)

6th August

First batch of 200 Reservists arrived at 3.00 a.m. Felixstowe detachment back. All kits and everything in Mess and Quarters packed. Reservists boots changed, clothing marked and deficiencies made up. Reservists practised in drill and musketry.
(*O Philby*)

Figure 1
Goojerat Barracks, Colchester. *Postcard*

After breakfast went to Colchester and to Goojerat Barracks (1st Somerset Light Infantry) and asked to enlist, waited all morning in the Orderly Room. After lunch posted to 'A' Company. Drew kit, made one or two friends; had tea, got bedding. As you will see by my address I have taken the shilling and am having quite an amusing time. I sleep on a bed comprising of things like carriage seats stuffed with coconut fibre, in a room with about twelve other men. I enlisted in a hurry because I want to go out to the front not muck about in barracks, but it isn't plumb certain now that anybody will go.
(*Edward Packe*)

7th August

Second batch of 500 Reservists arrived at 4.00 a.m. Clasp knives, pay books and ration bags issued. Platoons made up to War Strength, thus one loses one's best N.C.O.s on promotion. Extra men drafted to First Reinforcement and details.
(*O. Philby*)

Drew rest of kit and saw Commanding Officer, 'A' Company parade at 2.30 p.m. in Field Marching Order. Kit inspection by Mr. Bradshaw the Platoon Commander. Did up mufti, after tea had hair cut again.
(*Edward Packe*)

8th August

By the 8th (at 6.00 p.m.) the Battalion stood ready mobilized for war, awaiting orders to move.

Practically all the Transport horses caught influenza and many had to be changed.
(*O Philby*)

Rose 5.30 a.m. for early parade. Parade for drill in morning. Instruction in parts of rifle and issued with Field Service book.
(*Edward Packe*)

9th–16th August

The battalion spent from 9th to 16th August in Field Training and route marching

Platoon, Company and Battalion Training for Reservists, inoculation for Enteric.
(*O Philby*)

At present barrack life is one of the most amusing things I have ever struck. The men are so amazingly funny and they are always so cheery and one or two of them have got such priceless laughs that you can't help laughing too. There are some perfectly filthy rhymes written up in the 'rears' to while away the time spent striving with your inside. Every evening the old Regimental barber (who is an Irishman) holds a sort of gambling hell on the floor, illuminated by a guttering candle.

Our program is reveille at 5.30 a.m. parade (Company drill) 6.45 a.m. Breakfast at 8.00 a.m. Parade (Route march or manoeuvres) 9.30 a.m. We get back in time for lunch about 1.00 p.m. Foot and rifle inspection about 3.30 p.m. Tea at 5.00 p.m. Lights Out at 10.15 p.m, so you see we get half the day to ourselves and my word you want it after those route marches. I can scarcely bear braces on my shoulders when we get in, but I expect we shall get used to it by the time we go out.

I am very pleased with myself, getting steady pay, and if we go to the front we get £5 Blood Money, the Government offer you that, at the same time hoping that you don't live to claim it.

They are doing their best to get us into training we did the hell of a route march this morning, it isn't the distance, it's what you carry, including 120 rounds of 'ball', from which we are never parted now.

14th. Fire Instruction at 6.45 a.m. breakfast 7.15 a.m, parade Field Service Marching Order at 8.30 a.m. Short Route march. Rifle & foot inspection at midday. Tea at 4, get Pay (10/-)

16th. Parade at 8.00 a.m. for a route march, quite a hot one. Back at about 11.45 a.m., wash and clean rifle. Kit inspection after lunch. Pack up Sea Kit Bag. Read and talk, bed early.
(*Edward Packe*)

17th August

The 1st Somerset Light Infantry (with the 11th Infantry Brigade) left Colchester for Harrow, where the 4th Division had already begun to collect. The Battalion encamped on the playing fields of Harrow School. The 10th and 12th Infantry Brigade also arrived from Cromer and York

Camp on school football field, dry but on rather a slope. Delay in obtaining tents but finally pitched camp. I was detailed to command Divisional H.Q. guard of 30 men at the Kings Head. General Snow arrived at 4.00 p.m. Guard Room was an empty shop opposite the public house. Got electric light and water laid on and, with some trouble, got a fire to cook rations. The people gave the men food and we did fairly well.
(*O. Philby*)

Roused at 1.00 a.m., breakfast at 2.30 a.m., cleaned up barracks and paraded at 4.00 a.m. then entrained at 5.00 a.m. Reached Harrow at about 8.30 p.m. Dug 'rears' and refuse pit till 2.00 p.m. After tea got a Pass to visit friends. Back to camp and slept like the dead.
(*Edward Packe*)

18th–20th August

From the 18th to 20th inclusive the course of field training and route marching begun at Colchester was continued.

Musketry and route march. Very hot and some of the reservists had quite enough. Second inoculation but arm not so stiff as before. Permission granted to use the School bathing pond which was much appreciated.
(*O Philby*)

My platoon commander, Lieutenant Pretyman, asked me to take the Lance stripe. I was not very keen at first, but when older men in the platoon urged me to do so I agreed.
(*Arthur Cook*)

21st August

On the 21st the 4th Division left Harrow for Southampton, the Somerset Light

Figure 2
Troopship Braemar Castle. *Postcard*

Infantry entraining at 7.00 p.m. and arriving at the port at 11.30 p.m. embarked on the S.S. Braemar Castle at midnight.

> We left camp at 6.30 p.m. and marched to Sudbury Station. We are a happy crowd and sang at the tops of our voices. We could not have been in better spirits if we were all going on leave. People lined the streets and cheered us on our way. Reached Southampton Docks at 11.30 p.m. and embarked at midnight S.S. Braemar Castle and slept on the upper deck packed tightly together like a flock of sheep.
> (*Arthur Cook*)

22nd August

At 8.30 a.m. on the 22nd, the Battalion sailed from Southampton, reaching Havre at 7.00 p.m. But the tide was unsuitable for disembarkation and it was midnight before the troops set foot on shore.

> Embarked on S.S. Braemar Castle. This ship had been out of commission since the Boer War and had no fittings. Men packed very tight, officers three in a cabin. At 2.00 a.m. rest of Battalion arrived and horses and wagons slung down to the hold. Besides the Battalion the ship carried Brigade Headquarters, the East Lancs and half the Hants. Cast off at 8.30 a.m. and moved down Southampton Water followed by another transport. Every boat, yacht and fort wishing us 'Good Luck'. Passed a couple of Minesweepers. Captain of ship under sealed orders which were opened in Sandown Bay. We then made for Havre and the other transport to Boulogne. Sea smooth and weather excellent. Land sighted at 5.00 p.m. Off Havre at 8.30 p.m. but had to anchor to wait for a clear passage in. Picked up French pilot and entered harbour 10.00 p.m. Berthed at midnight and took some time disembarking.
> (*O Philby*)

> We embarked at 1.00 a.m. Did manage to get some sleep. Sailed at 8.30 a.m. Had breakfast of bully beef and biscuit. Passed Isle of Wight at 11.00 a.m. Had some lunch. Looked round ship; saw propeller shaft, stoke hole etc. Sighted land first at about 5.15 p.m. and took pilot aboard at about 7.00 p.m. Not enough water so lay off till about 10.30 p.m. Landed at Havre at 11.30 p.m. Got to Rest Camp at 4.00 a.m. We were so crammed on board that we couldn't get our feet out straight.
> (*Edward Packe*)

> The French pilot made many bad shots at berthing the ship, so we could not start unloading the ship till about 12.30 a.m. We were met in the docks with cries of "A bas Guillaume," "Couper la gorge," and other bloodthirsty shouts. Also "Heep! Heep! Hooray!"
> (*G Prideaux*)

23rd August

At about 2.00 a.m. on the 23rd, the Somerset Light Infantry marched to the rest camp six miles from Havre, a painful march, uphill, in great heat.

Ultimately left the quay at 2.00 a.m. marching through town and up a steep hill to the rest camp. Arrived 4.30 a.m finding the camp very dirty, and rather fruity, when the sun got up. Hargreaves and I were sent to the station to get orders about our entrainment. Went on cycles and found it very hot in the town.
(*O Philby*)

We are now on French soil and had a great welcome from the French people. We marched from the Docks to a camp on the top of a hill, which we reached about 3.30 a.m., and anchored down for a sleep. We were given two Oxo tablets and emergency rations. We were told that on no account should we use these unless told to do so by an officer. We cooked our own meal of bacon, bread and tea and were told to get as much rest as possible.
(*Arthur Cook*)

We had quite a triumphant procession the inhabitants cheering and giving us flowers in exchange for the men's badges. A breach of discipline which could not be countenanced.
(*W. Watson*)

Rest and numerous camp duties occupied the men during the day.
Whole Battalion rendezvoused at station at 10.00 p.m. Fatigue parties and drivers loaded vehicles and horses whilst remainder of Battalion slept on platforms. This was not such a good system as in England, where only those actually required for loading work were sent to the station until required for entrainment.

Paraded 8.00 p.m. and marched to the station through a cheering French crowd. Long wait while wagons and. horses were put into the trucks. Being a different size to the English trucks, it was a bit of a job getting them fitted in. Forty men to a wagon which does not give them much room. Brigade Headquarters turned up unexpectedly to go in our train so Taylor, Pretyman, Newton, Macbryan and myself had to travel with the Mess baskets of stores. Unfortunately we did not have the keys and the baskets were locked.
(*O. Philby*)

Men are packed in cattle trucks, but make the best of it as usual, imitating the bellowing and bleating of oxen and sheep. To these sounds we steam out of the station.
(*W Watson*)

During the evening the Colonel read to us the King's message to his troops also telling us that not many hours distant we should be facing the enemy. We cheered the King and country and the noise we made frightened the Colonel's horse which reared up and threw him but he was soon all right. We had orders that we were going up country that night. Nearly all the men were anxious at the time because three men had broke camp and had not returned and we all thought of disgrace so soon; but I'm glad to say they returned just as we were moving from camp. (*Arthur Green*)

[This paper is to be considered by each soldier as confidential, and to be kept in his Active Service Pay Book.]

You are ordered abroad as a soldier of the King to help our French comrades against the invasion of a common enemy. You have to perform a task which will need your courage, your energy, your patience. Remember that the honour of the British Army depends on your individual conduct. It will be your duty not only to set an example of discipline and perfect steadyness under fire but also to maintain the most friendly relations with those whom you are helping in this struggle. The operations in which you are engaged will, for the most part, take place in a friendly country, and you can do your own country no better service than in showing yourself in France and Belgium in the true character of a British soldier.

Be invariably courteous, considerate and kind. Never do anything likely to injure or destroy property, and always look upon looting as a disgraceful act. You are sure to meet a welcome and to be trusted; your conduct must justify that welcome and that trust. Your duty cannot be done unless your health is sound. So keep constantly on your guard against any excesses. In this new experience you may find temptations both in wine and women. You must entirely resist both temptations, and, while treating all women with perfect courtesy, you should avoid any intimacy.

Do your duty bravely.
Fear God.
Honour the King.
KITCHENER,
Field Marshal.

Chapter Two

Le Cateau
24th–26th August

24th August

Loading the whole Battalion to one train took until 1.00 a.m. and the Somersets then left Havre station at 2.00 a.m. The journey from Havre was none too comfortable, as the troops were packed in cattle trucks, and travelling all day in a scorching sun under such conditions would have damped the ardour of anyone but the British soldier

> The first official despatch received by the War Office from Sir John French stated that "The 4th Division commenced its detrainment at Le Cateau on Sunday the 23rd, and, by the morning of the 25th, eleven battalions and a brigade of artillery with Divisional Staff were available for service. I [Sir John] ordered General Snow to take up a position with his right south of Solesmes, his left resting on the Cambrai-Le Cateau road, south of La Chapelle."
> (*History*)

> I certainly did not see much prospect of getting any sleep with someone else's boots in my face and we began to feel rather uncomfortable as the day had been hot and the pave had touched up our feet. There were heated discussions as to where we were going, but after a 20 minutes rest at Rouen, where we had some excellent coffee with a nip of brandy in it (at which, by the way, the men scoffed) the popular opinion was that we were going to somewhere near Lille. Bully beef and biscuits did not seem at all appetizing in a very dirty railway carriage, but we were better off than the men who I am afraid must have suffered terribly from a blazing sun in open railway trucks. Voisey, of my Company, was taken off the train sick some time in the afternoon. This man afterwards wrote a letter to the paper describing all the trials he had been through on the retreat from Mons.
> (*W. Whittuck*)

The train halted at Rouen where we were given black coffee, which we did not like. We went on past Yeotot, Mettetot, Barentin and Busigny and at 6.00 p.m. reached Le Cateau, feeling very cramped and untidy. Forty of us, in full marching order had spent 17 hours crammed in each cattle truck. We then marched eight miles to a village which we reached about 10.00 p.m., and I slept the night in a shed. The leave atmosphere has evaporated but we are all very chirpy. What is happening? No one has any idea.
(*Arthur Cook*)

Detrained at Le Cateau at 5.00 p.m. Ordered to move to ****, but met on way by staff officer in motorcar who directed battalion to Briastre. Adjutant being sent to 4th Division H.Q at Inchy for orders, which were to occupy Briastre. Battalion arrived about 8.00 p.m. and 'A' and 'B' Companies furnished outposts on hills north of village.

We detrained at Le Cateau about 6.00 p.m. and had a lot of trouble in getting the men out, as so many of them had taken off their equipment and puttees in the great heat. We were told that we were to go into billets at a little village about two miles out, but heard no real news though there were some rather disquieting rumours about Army Headquarters having to be moved back from Le Cateau. We started off, but had not gone more than a mile before we were told to branch off the main road, destination unknown. We marched over what seemed miles of pave and the men seemed pretty well done, though they certainly kept well together as they were evidently feeling all the weight they had to carry on a hot evening. Eventually we reached a small village called Briastre about 10.00 p.m. Hunter-Weston passing us on the road and congratulating us on our marching. I was sent on with two sections to block all roads leading into the village from the northeast, but did not think much of it, as I had heard that the Germans were about 200 miles away and we imagined that we had the whole of the French Army and our two corps between us and them. Outposts were eventually put out by 'A' and 'B' Companies and I returned to billets with my men about 11.00 p.m. looking forward to a good square meal and a good night's rest as I felt that I had not had much sleep lately. Thoyts came in with rather a grave face soon after I returned. He said that German cavalry were reported within five miles and that we were to be ready to move at a moment's notice. It seemed almost impossible but we all lay down on the stone floor of the kitchen, after having had some coffee and bread, just as we were.
(*W Whittuck*)

The situation late on August 24th was that, after holding the Germans at Mons, the B.E.F and French were falling back in a southwesterly direction towards Paris. The 1st Corps under General Haig was able to march according to plan, but General Smith Dorian's 2nd Corps found itself in an exposed position, as the French cavalry, which were to cover his flank, had not appeared. To continue the retreat would have meant that his troops would be at the mercy of enemy artillery and cavalry. After consulting with General Allenby, the cavalry commander, he decided to make a stand in the Le Cateau area to enable his command to regroup.

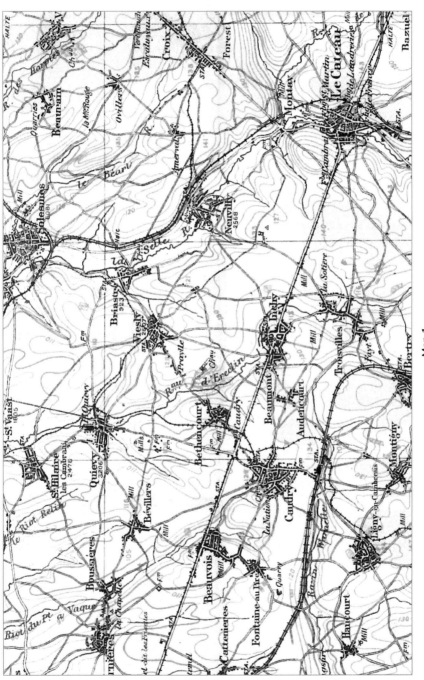

Map 1
Le Cateau

At the same time the 4th Division, was in the process of arriving from Le Havre, had begun deploying and had come into contact with the enemy. General Snow agreed, that as his force was already involved, he had no choice but to make a stand. The Division however was not fully assembled and lacked its support troops, (cavalry, ambulances, engineers, heavy artillery and ammunition train).

25th August

The 4th Division was disposed to cover the retirement of the 2nd Corps and the 19th Infantry Brigade from Mons. The retention of Solesmes until the Corps had passed was absolutely essential, as the town was the apex of roads running from the north southwards, down which the troops must pass

During the early evening 4th Division issued orders to its brigades to withdraw during the night to positions selected for them on the left of the 3rd Division – the 11th and 12th Brigades to hold the line Fontaine au Pire-Wambaix (respectively), the 10th Brigade to be in reserve at Haucourt. (*History*)

Moved at 4.00 a.m. at short notice and marched to Solesmes, occupied position south of village. Heard heavy firing to northwest and about 9.00 p.m. withdrew to a position north of Viesly. Enemy's cavalry was seen about 6.00 p.m. south of Solesmes and this position was shelled in a desultory manner. At 5.00 p.m. all vehicles were withdrawn under Brigade arrangements and at about 9.00 p.m. the order was given to withdraw the troops. Half Battalion H.Q. and 'C' and 'D' Companies marched with the Brigade at about 10.00 p.m. Remainder of H.Q. and 'A' and 'B' companies formed rearguard of the Brigade and withdrew at 11.00 p.m.

Reconnoitre Solesmes with Piasmon, who, usually taciturn, unburdens himself, to the extent that he had been preparing for this campaign all his life. Cannot say the same for myself, hunting and polo have commanded some of my attention as well as war. In Solesmes see the first signs that we are in for a retreat. Local French Territorial Regiment marches out away from the enemy. Streets are barricaded. Civilians hastily collecting their goods in small bundles and pushing off in southerly direction. From our position we can see farms, villages bursting into flames on the heights above Solesmes. Dangers of war are becoming unpleasantly close.
(*W Watson*)

Got two hours sleep. Turned out at 3.30 a.m. and Battalion assembled. Maps issued and the Battalion marched towards Solesmes. Halted in a brickfield and heard heavy rifle and gunfire somewhere out in front. Went forward to Pigeon Blanc to reconnoitre an advanced position. Stream of ambulances and French troops retiring. The streets of Solesmes barricaded. Firing came nearer and the gunfire became continuous. Informed we were in for a retirement. Afterwards

found we were opposed by five army corps and not two as the French thought. More troops passed us and we began to dig ourselves in. Had a pot at an aeroplane but had no luck, though it was bagged later by somebody else. 12th Brigade on our left and some guns came and took up a position close to us. At midday a thunderstorm came up and we got soaked by the heavy rain. Ground undulating and covered with turnips, mangolds and cut and standing corn. Trenches got very muddy with the rain. Trail of fugitives from the villages in front came hurrying past us all day. Battalion H.Q. is in village of Viesly. Solesmes shelled but only a few came our way. Before darkness came on I could see masses of German infantry coming over the ridges north of Solesmes. A village on our left was set on fire and kept burning the whole night. Our advanced trenches shelled a bit just before the guns stopped for the night but no damage. After posting sentries and an advanced post out on the track in front, there was nothing to do but wait and try to get warm. During the early part of the night, the 12th Brigade in the trenches on our left burst into fire over an Uhlan (German Lancer) patrol, who retired very hurriedly leaving one or two behind. We received no orders but our patrols reported all clear in front. About midnight got an order to find Prowse and tell him to retire at once as 'C' and 'D' Companies had been gone some time and unnoticed by us. Company reassembled and retired to Viesly and then through it.
(*O Philby*)

Managed to get a bit of bully beef, which I shared with Montgomery. Hunter-Weston then arrived and said that we had a glorious task in front of us – 'a strategic retirement to a position round St. Quentin'. Our faces rather fell, as it all seemed so different from what we had expected. We were told that we were to occupy a position southwest of Solesmes with a view to helping the retirement of especially the 5th Division, which had been rather hard pressed. We had no tools but managed to dig ourselves fairly well in with the light entrenching tool, but we had a long stretch of ground to hold and it was difficult to get a good field of fire in root fields. About 3.00 p.m. we began to wonder when we were going to get a meal, as the men only had their emergency rations with them and of course there were no orders about eating them. We found that the turnips were something to suck and quenched our thirst a bit. It had been raining hard all the afternoon, but we did not put on greatcoats as we thought we might move at any moment. The rain stopped now and we had our first experience of shelling, but the shells went over us as they were meant for a battery in rear. It grew dusk now really was a wonderful sight to see the enemy's guns firing on the opposite slope. Yatman came up and said we were to retire and rejoin the remainder of the Battalion. This we managed to do by taking a difficult cross-country route to Quievy where we found the Colonel. We could not get on to the road however as it was blocked by a cavalry train. Yatman and I walked down the road and managed to wake the drivers and get them on the move.
(*W Whittuck*)

At 6.45 a.m. we could hear fairly rapid gunfire in the distance. The morale of the boys is excellent and looking forward to the fight. We advanced up sloping ground over a harvest field and entrenched ourselves with our entrenching tools. About 9.45 a.m. a German aeroplane came to have a look at us. My section was ordered to fire five rounds rapid at it, which we carried out as taught on the barrack square. I do not suppose we went near it, for it made off as if nothing had happened. Any way, we opened our account with the Kaiser, which gave us some satisfaction.
(*Arthur Cook*)

After about six hours rest the Somersets formed up at about 6.00 a.m. and marched about a mile out of the village, picking up their patrols as they went. The Somersets got down into a dip and proceeded to entrench themselves. I suppose it was the artillery fire going on that brought down the rain. We could see an artillery duel going on in front of us about five or six miles ahead. The rain came on and it came down pretty thick. But our men could not be done and while it was raining they took off their shirts and continued digging the trenches. They had nothing on but their trousers, boots and stockings and thus stripped to the waist worked through the rain. You could see the steam coming from their bodies as they worked away. We put the barbed wire entanglements about 50 yards in front of the trenches in case of any cavalry attacks.
(*Archibald Miles, Bath Chronicle*)

From:	4th Division
To:	11th Brigade
Time:	0930

Take back your 2nd line transport to Ligny

From:	11th Division
To:	Somerset Light Infantry
Time:	1140

Your report received. The Hampshires and East Lancs are holding ridge 1 mile SE of Soleesmes. The Rifle Brigade are now up and moving into position just NW of Briastre when they will be able to support you. They have order to hold Solesmes-Briastre road. Am sending you cook's wagon.

From:	11th Division
To:	4th Division
Time:	11340

Following received from Somerset Light Infantry. Major Compton reports at 12.30 Khaki columns estimated at one brigade retiring from Romeries-Solesmes road also one company retiring on Pigeon Blanc road....

August 26th

After a continuous night march from Briastre 1 1/2 miles south of Solesmes, the 11th Infantry Brigade halted for 1 1/2 hours at the northern end of Fontaine au Pire at 2.45 a.m. on 26th August 1914. At 4.14 a.m. as the Brigade was about to resume its march, rifle machine gun and shellfire was opened on the outposts west of the village of Beauvois. While the Rifle Brigade held off this attack to the north and northwest, the Somerset Light Infantry were pushed forward to the southern end of Beauvois to hold of the enemy to the northeast and to ensure the safe passage of all wheeled vehicles to the east and then to the south. The direct roads south from the halting place being impassable owing to the wet.

Under cover of these two Battalions the other two Battalions moved south and took up a position on the ridge of which Carrieres (The Quarry) 1/2 mile southwest of the village of Fontaine au Pire is the centre. All the transport was successfully got away, but owing to the necessity of having to stick to the roads the 1st Line transport had to go a long way round to Selvigny, which it reached safely in due course.

(*11th Infantry Brigade Diary*)

The Battalion moved during night to Fontaine Au Pire, the two rear companies arriving there about 2.30 a.m. The C.O. was with these two companies and being given a free hand as to their disposal by the Brigadier, decided, after a reconnaissance to entrench a position about 800 yards north of Ligny. This was commenced at about 4.00 a.m. The other two companies were dispatched with the remainder of the Brigade on a line east of Fontaine au Pire under the G.O.C.

Major Compton commanding
  – 'C' Company (Major Thoyts) holding north edge of quarries
  – 'D' Company (less 2 platoons) under Captain Yatman, and
  Machine Gun Section holding eastern edge of quarries.
  – 2 Platoons 'D' Company holding road between Fontaine au Pire
    and quarries.
A company of the East Lancs occupied the western end of the quarries.

The troops taking whatever cover was possible, the surrounding country being very open. A glacis-like slope, which provided the only fair field of fire, led up to where the companies were extended.

Colonel Swayne commanding
  – 'A' and 'B' companies north of Ligny.

We had only reached Fontaine au Pire when we were ordered back again to Beauvois where 'C' Company was sent off to occupy some gardens, as reports had come in, that the enemy's cavalry were moving up all the roads in force. My Company was at present kept in reserve but Montgomery's and my platoons were soon sent off to occupy some gardens from which we could see nothing, but the men were rather nervous at this their first experience of shrapnel fire. The morning was very misty and it looked rather as if the Germans had

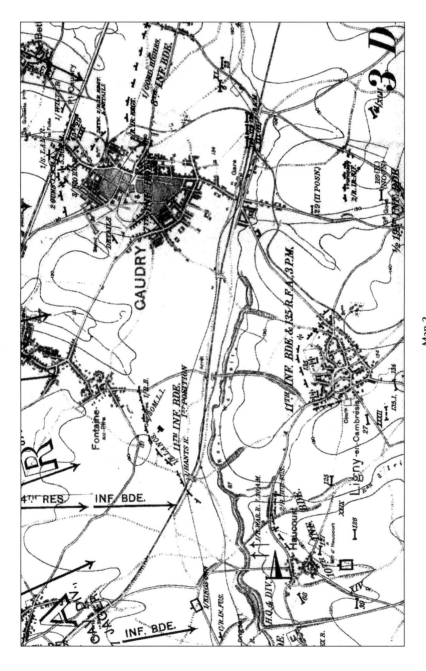

Map 2
Caudry

surprised us as we certainly (who knew nothing) did not expect to be followed up quite so closely. I was eventually ordered by Hargreaves to withdraw to the road. He said that the remainder of the Company had retired and that we should go on and find out where we were to join up. I was to gradually leave the village, leaving posts at each turning which were not to retire till I had got clear of the next one. As I was retiring, I joined up with some of the Hampshires, but when I got to the top of the hill out of the village I could see nothing, though the shell and rifle fire was pretty heavy. This was about 8.30 a.m. I continued to retire down the road but could see nothing of the remainder of the Battalion, so I imagined they must have come up into the firing line. I tried the left of the road first but only fell in with an Irish Regiment that was retreating very rapidly. I then crossed over to the other side. About 10.30 a.m I met Yatman who told me to take my few men up to the supporting line. There I found Sutton and Pretyman with a mixture of men from all Companies. He did not know what had happened but our orders were to hold this position to cover the retirement of the rest of the Battalion. I was very glad to get some bully. As the sun was very hot we could have all slept if the noise had not been so great.
(*W. Whittuck*)

Under cover of the fire of the 1st Battalion, Hampshire Regiment the two advanced Battalions retired on La Carriere. The Somerset Light Infantry (1 1/2 Companies) occupying the eastern end of the quarry while a Company of the East Lancs occupied the western end. The Somersets prolonged their own line from La Carriere to the southeast, sending a Company back towards Ligny to entrench a position North of that town.

The Brigade having thus established itself on the Carriere ridge the Companies of the Somersets and East Lancs were recalled from their covering positions north of Ligny and formed local reserves on the west and east flanks of the Carrieres position
(*11th Infantry Brigade Diary*)

At 5.30 a.m. heavy artillery fire was opened on the quarries position, which was very exposed and entirely untrenched. Under cover of this fire (our own guns had not yet come into action) German infantry and machine guns advanced to close range. Some of the latter moved into the village of Fontaine au Pire and enfiladed the Quarries position. Majors Compton and Thoyts (the 2 senior officers present) were both wounded.

At 7.00 a.m. the G.O.C. ordered 'A' and 'B' Companies forward to move to a wood just south of the Quarries to be in reserve. On the way portions of these companies were diverted by the G.O.C. to the position held by 'C' and 'D' Companies. As they reached the firing line German skirmishers were seen about 700 yards away advancing and taking cover behind the corn-stooks, which dotted the fields. About two platoons reached the wood south of the quarries.

At dawn passed through Beauvois and found rest of Battalion sleeping on pavement. Continued through Fontaine au Pire towards Ligny en Cambresi to take up position at the top of the ridge, I found I had to go some way over the other side to get a field of fire. 'A' Company south of the road and 'B' Company north of it. Positions on slopes covered with corn and turnips and very wet and muddy. Found Prideaux who had his transport somewhere close to hand, who presented me with the tail end of a box of sardines, which I quickly finished. Heavy gun and rifle fire broke out against 12th Brigade on a ridge on our left. C.O. ordered us to advance to the Fontaine ridge and hold that. Advanced in successive lines 200 yards apart and crossed the stream and railway without loss. I think though there were a few shells coming over. Jones Mortimer pointed out the front and he and I nearly stopped one there, a couple of bullets going under my foot. Arriving a bit lively on the ridge by this time, particularly as the Brigadier insisted on riding round in full view, rather giving the show away. Macbryan and his platoon came up on my left and Bennett and his machine guns tucked himself in a quarry and started in great style. We could not find much of a target and the Huns started a systematic traversing fire on the ridge.

I suddenly thought the world had fallen on me, being caught by a bullet which rather knocked me endways for a bit. I got my equipment off and had a drink and began to take notice again, but could not move for a bit.
(*O Philby*)

At 7.45 a.m. three shells burst over us, in quick succession, and hit three men and alarmed the rest horribly. We all got our heads down behind our head cover, scraped up with our entrenching tools, just enough to stop a bullet, if you throw the earth well out to the front. I had just borrowed a tool from a man, and scraped up a bit before the firing began. This cover is no good against shrapnel, which bursts overhead. Luckily, after those three shells, the Germans fired on the supports; otherwise we should have been wiped out in a quarter of an hour. The Germans had the range plumb. Then the Rifle Brigade retired across our front and got fired at by some of us, not knowing who they were. Then there was a lull. At about 8.45 a.m. a skirmishing line came across the road, in front of the German guns, and I gave my first fire order about five minutes later. 'Enemy advancing 1500 – distribute fire' I don't think we hit anyone as the range was very long and I couldn't see the bullets strike anywhere to correct the range. I shouted back to the machine gun, who had a range-finder to give the ranges, but I couldn't make them hear. Two German guns then walked quietly along the distant road and came into action with the others behind them. I tried to fire on them, but it was 1800 or 2000 yards, and again I could make no one hear behind me. I saw the guns come into action and the observer in his sort of scaffold arrangement. I could see him through my field-glasses turn and shout when a shell pitched short. A few more men were hit by shrapnel and the nerve of the others shaken badly (which is what shrapnel is for). Then a machine gun started on our right and hit a few more, and I looked at my watch wondering how long we could stay there. So far very few infantry came at us, mostly going to the left of us where the rifle and machine-gun fire was very heavy.
(*G R Parr*)

I had not gone far when a bullet struck the earth a yard in front of me and nearly blinded me with dirt. That was a narrow escape. We continued to advance in extended order in spite of heavy machine gun fire, up a slope into line with a hedge where we lay down and opened fire on the advancing Germans. Wave after wave fell under our carefully aimed fire as taught on the ranges. The only difference was now we had something alive to fire at which made it more interesting for, strangely enough, none of us minded killing another human being. Here we were giving the enemy Hell, but as soon as a gap was torn in their ranks it was filled up from behind. We too were getting casualties for men were being killed right and left of me.
(*Arthur Cook*)

We got down between two fields and took off our greatcoats, which we had been wearing owing to the heavy rain all night. Before we could get them packed in our bags, bang, bang go other shells right over our heads. The position was getting rather warm. 'Come on' was the next order and out into the open we went into a hail of shells and bullets. 'Up the front of the bank' was the next order. Oh it was shocking to hear and see the shells bursting all around us. We could see the German artillery away on our right, but our artillery had got lost or strayed. We had no artillery to reply to the Germans and no ambulance to pick up the wounded. However we took up a position and started.

My God, we could see thousands of Germans swarming out of a wood straight in front of us about a thousand yards away. We started dropping them like wheat before the scythe but still they came. At last I heard the call to my right for an ambulance, but there was none there, so the only thing to be done was to crawl or roll for safety and our men started to go back, one or two at a time, wounded. But let it be understood that, it was not the thousands of infantry that were doing the damage, it was the German shrapnel. They had the range splendidly. But what a sensation to see the shells bursting all around us and expecting to get your head blown away at any minute.

We kept on dropping the German infantry until I felt something strike me on the back of the head. I knew no more for some time. Then I heard someone say 'Go for it.' but I was too dazed to do anything. Soon, however, I started to crawl for safety. A shell burst a few yards in front of me and caused me to stop for some time. I had to crawl on my stomach for the last 30 feet to safety. Then the orderly started to put on my field dressing, but before he had finished we had to retire, as we could not hold the position any longer.
(*Thomas Tadd – Bath Chronicle*)

They came on like a great grey moving hedge the men firing, as Germans usually do, with their rifles on their hips. When they were about 250 yards from us the order was given to open fire. And then the Somersets rifles began to whistle. The first few volleys made the enemy shiver and gaps here and there began to appear like shords in an untidy hedge. We pulled them up but, as the enemy were in vastly superior numbers, we had orders to retire and fell back a

good way. The Somersets withstood the onslaught splendidly but I'm afraid we lost heavily. While we were descending the slope of the hill the fire was terrific, in fact those who had gone through the Boer War said it was like the whole three years of the South African campaign rolled into an hour or so. Our chaps kept dropping and some of the sights were awful. I can vividly recall quite a youngster Private – saying to me as we descended the slope 'I don't think the beggars could hit me if they tried.' At that instant a shell caught him in the forehead and his head was shattered.
(*Thomas Parkman, Wells Journal*)

We were waiting in a village to the north of Cambrai after an all night march during which we did not see any Germans, and at 6.00 a.m. we marched into position. Two minutes later I was rolling over the ridge, shot in the head by a shrapnel shell. It burst right over the top of where I was lying. A couple of inches more and I would have been blown to pieces. As it is I have a hole just above my right temple. My regiment is nearly all killed, wounded or missing. It was simply terrible to witness it. Although our forces lost a lot the German losses were three or four times more. It was impossible to miss them, but as fast as one lot had gone under there were thousands more to take their places. The work of their big guns is magnificent but their infantry is almost useless at shooting. We'll beat them if men will roll up to take the place of those who are killed or wounded.
(*Private Evans, Bath Chronicle*)

At about 9.30 a.m. Major Collins (East Lancs) and Captain Yatman conferred and decided that, owing to the enfilade machine gun fire, the position at the quarries was untenable. Measures were therefore taken to withdraw to the railway embankment, which ran along the valley between Ligny and Fontaine.

So, leaving a single platoon behind under Lieutenant Taylor, the Battalion, in short rushes, retired south of the railway, towards Ligny. The platoon being in an exposed position lost about 38 of 50 N.C.O.s and men. Lieutenant Taylor was wounded and fell into the hands of the enemy.

The remainder of the Battalion reserve retired to the railway embankment and to the north of Ligny and took up positions to cover the retirement of the Rifle Brigade and the platoon of 'C' Company. No fire was opened from these position however as it was not possible to distinguish friend from foe on the Quarries Ridge. The Brigade had now established a line on the Carriere Ridge running just north of the railway line.

Just previous to the decision to retire, a German patrol waving a white flag evidently meant to invite the Somerset men to surrender, endeavoured to work round the right flank of the Battalion. "The men asked me what to do. 'Fire on the beggars, range 500 yards.' Germans drop hastily."
(*W Watson*)

The machine gun then enfiladed us on both flanks and more messages came to ask about retiring. I told them we were going to stay where we were.

They shouted up to me that there was nobody left on our left flank and that our supports had gone. At about 12.30 p.m. I shouted out that we would retire, and we started to crawl back the 50 yards to the old quarry. After some distance a man said to me, 'They're getting hit, let's run for it'; so we ran the last fifteen yards and dropped down over the bank. Out of 49 that I took into action I had only 12 left. 37 were killed or wounded, so that there was no disgrace in retiring.

(*G R Parr*)

We hung on in this position until about 1.00 p.m. when they suddenly opened a heavy shrapnel fire on us (absolutely perfect range). A small part of our men got up and ran but I am sorry to say were mostly knocked out. Their attitudes struck one as absolutely grotesque, but the moaning and cries of pain were terrible, as we could do nothing for them except bandage a few up and leave them.

(*W Whittuck*)

We had taken up all our supports outside the town into a dip about 80 yards wide. This was a long ditch shaped depression and it afforded natural protection with a bank about 9 ft high between us and the firing. Men from our half battalion had gone to fill up gaps in the Rifle Brigade before the enemy located us in the dip and began to drop shells near us. As men were hit, out in the firing line, we got them back to shelter and more supports went up to take their place. The enemy observed these movements and their artillery sent about a dozen shells at us. The first shells went over us but the range was brought down until the shells pitched two or three feet from the edge of the bank beyond which we were sheltering.

Just in front of the dip and affording useful cover for our supports to rush up to the firing line was a little farmhouse. A couple of German shells on the farmhouse levelled it to the ground, and after that, as the supports went up the enemy shells dropped among them. We got a lot of wounded back some so badly wounded that we had to leave them when we retired, as we had lost our Maltese cart with the stretchers in. Only the wounded that were able to walk got back with us. Eventually the order came for us to retire.

All this time I had been in the dip except when I was called forward to the firing line to bandage wounded men. My brother Gilbert and I were working together when the order to retire was given. There was a roadway leading from the enemy towards the dip and they must have had a maxim gun trained down it, for bullets came flying along. My brother made a bid to get across the road and made it all right. I wondered how I could cross in safety and eventually I rolled clean across the road and down the bank the other side. The enemy were now advancing quickly towards us. My brother left me and returned across the road to the wounded we had left. I was now on my own and made a rush up the bank behind me. Then I had to dash about 300 yards of a turnip

field. As luck would have it there was a little thicket of green stuff in the field growing about 6 feet high and offering perfect cover. As I made towards it they must have trained the maxim on me as I heard the bullets whistling by me and about half a dozen passed between my legs and took the soil up right in front of me. But I reached the green stuff and was lost to sight. Eventually, on the far side, the ground fell away and I was under cover.
(*Archibald Miles, Stretcher Bearer*)

Later on I got the order passed on from Watson to retire as the troops on the left had already gone. I handed the platoon over to Sergeant Ellis and told him to take it back, saying I would get back later. They got away fairly well, I think, and after waiting a bit, I started to crawl after them but got such violent cramp in both legs that I had to stop. The Huns had seen us going and were giving us a bit of a hard time. After waiting a bit longer I got up and thought that I would try and run back. I got over the crest of the hill about 70 yards down the other slope when I caught another in the left shoulder and turned about three somersaults. I then saw a good many of the men being hit as they retired, and Taylor also went down with one in his leg. I did not think the place very healthy and started off again but did not get very far before I got a chunk of shell in the leg. However there were no bones broken and after another rest. I managed to reach the railway embankment where I met Newton. Crossing the stream I came across Prowse who was forming a line with what he could collect of the Company. I picked up the remainder of the platoon and handed them over to him saying I would go back to the village and get tied up. Started towards Ligny but found it pretty heavy going through the turnips. Outside the village I met a stretcher bearer who gave me a drink and helped me to a dressing station fixed up in a local school where he patched me up and, incidentally, cut my clothes to ribbons to do it. Found some of my platoon and more came in later.
(*O. Philby*)

A little distance away was a railway and our 'A' Company was keeping the embankment until our men got back or the Germans should come over the dip. Two guns of our artillery were near a village on the left, towards which I was making. I caught up with some of our supports. In the meantime the German guns had come round and were in a position almost flanking that occupied by our guns. Seeing our stragglers coming in the German artillery shortened their range and sent shrapnel over them. Very few of ours, however, got hit and I was one of the unlucky ones. I got hit in the neck just to the left of the vertebrae. A quarter of an inch nearer the centre would have killed me. As it was I was not hit out but numbed for some time and I made off to the village near our guns, where I got bandaged up. A few more of our wounded came back there to a church which had been converted to a hospital.
(*Archibald Miles*)

The transport less 6 S.A.A. (Small Arms Ammunition) carts marched south under the railway to Ligny, on the way supplying water to 'A' Company also food. The road from Haucourt-Ligny was blocked with artillery, three deep, galloping into action. On reaching Ligny village we parked in the street and started to cook some breakfast. From there we moved into a valley between Ligny and Montigny, where we came across the Cavalry division, halted in mass. We moved to Caullery, where we just managed to get some breakfast before the village was shelled. The wounded, those who could walk, now commenced to dribble back, also a number of stragglers, who were sent back! From Caullery I tripped off to Clary, not knowing where to go as I had received no orders.

In Clary I found a regular pandemonium, the village street was blocked by ammunition columns trying to get forward and ambulances trying to get away. Added to this the street was littered with stretchers with wounded on them and any number of stragglers were running about, half-demented with the idea that the whole force had been wiped out by the Germans. Into the middle of this turmoil strolled the transport of the Somerset L.I. making the confusion worse. (*G Prideaux, Transport Officer*)

At about 3.00 p.m, the 5th Division having retired from Caudry, it was seen that to hold the Carriere position any longer would lead to the Brigade being taken in reverse. In accordance, therefore, with Divisional instructions the Brigade made preparations to retire to Ligny. This retirement was carefully organised with close cooperation between infantry and artillery, the latter taking up positions in and to the west of Ligny ready to engage the enemy's artillery and infantry and to cover the retirement. The infantry, with the Rifle Brigade on the position as rearguard, was formed up in lines on the dead ground south of the Ravin Warnelle, where on the command being given it moved off in good order towards the village of Ligny. Each Battalion was given a separate objective viz; the Hampshires to the west of the village, Somersets to the east end of village, the Rifle Brigade following towards the left centre. The shrapnel fire on our troops was very severe notwithstanding the support given by the guns. There were a good number of casualties but considering the way the whole ground was plastered with shrapnel bullets it was surprising that the casualties were not greater. As soon as the rearguard quitted the Carriere position the German Infantry which up to that time had kept themselves carefully concealed advanced in large numbers on the Caudry side of that position. They afforded excellent targets to the artillery and their formations were speedily broken up by shrapnel fire

On arrival at Ligny the battalions reformed in the locations that had been allocated to them and took up defence in front of their respective portions of the village. Shortly after the Brigade had established itself at Ligny an attack was made on the east and northeast of the village by German infantry. This attack was pushed in twice but on each occasion was repulsed with heavy loss (*11th Brigade Diary*)

The remains of the Somersets reached Ligny at about 4.00 p.m. There they

reorganized and took up their positions at the eastern end of the village. Casualties were collected and placed in the church. Unfortunately the Divisional Field Ambulances and other Divisional troops, excepting Artillery, had been held back by G.H.Q., and were at St. Quentin. The wounded could not be evacuated, though Captain Holden, R.A.M.C., attached, managed to collect a few carts in which he placed some of the worst cases and dispatched them southwards towards St. Quentin. For some inexplicable reason these carts were turned back to Ligny under the direction of a staff officer. All these wounded subsequently fell into the hands of the enemy.
(*History*)

When we got back to the village we were collected into the village square and the C.O. made a speech. He said the French had supposed to come to our aid, but hadn't, so we had to defend the village to the last man, and were to take off our packs and use them as head cover. Although we had only four guns they worked the most awful havoc on the Germans, as our shells are so much better than theirs and although their shooting is wonderfully accurate, their infantry fire is not so good.
(*Edward Packe*)

The order was given to hold Ligny at all costs and defensive measures were taken. Just before 4 p.m. the village was heavily shelled and a storm of rifle fire broke out on the right of the 4th Division. Battalion after battalion of German infantry was launched against the village from the northeast, their skirmishers advancing with great dash and taking advantage of every scrap of cover, the standing corn and stooks affording them great opportunities. But none of their attacks could be pushed home, the British artillery and the machine guns firing point-blank, taking a terrible toll of the enemy's troops. At 400 yards from the British line the German attack broke down. Again and again the enemy tried to storm Ligny, but meeting shrapnel and rapid rifle fire, the German attack melted away, and seeing persistence useless they gave up the attempt, leaving the 11th Infantry Brigade in undisputed possession of the village.
(*History*)

Tried to get an ambulance but none about and I believe our divisional ambulance is still in England. Macbryan came in with one in his leg. Got hold of a farm cart which was soon full up with wounded and started off south with the idea of picking up an ambulance somewhere. Had got cold by now and was shivering violently and as stiff as a board. Met some of the Battalion under Compton with whom was our doctor, Holden, who said it was no use going back further and he would form a hospital in Ligny, so back we trekked under him. We now returned to the school from which we had just come and then met Freestun trying to collect bits of the Brigade together. Had to be carried into the school where I was lucky enough to get a bed upstairs, where I promptly went to sleep. In the evening the village was shelled but the school was not hit,

though there were some near things. Taylor, Hargreaves, Macbryan, myself, Halls and Baxter of the Hants, Foljambe and Lane of the Rifle Brigade, Collins and Hooper of the East Lancs and Armitage, a gunner were upstairs and the men were below and in the church. Stragglers came through the village the whole night but the Germans never entered it. I heard after that they thought they had knocked out the whole British Army that day and could not collect in time the mass of troops that they had deployed for the purpose
(*O Philby*)

Then the German infantry advanced again in mass but was mowed down by our magazine fire, during the whole day the Germans were advancing and retiring, and still we held the ground. There was not a man in my section hit till about five o'clock, when the Germans opened upon us with their machine guns. This was about the time when Major Thoyts was severely wounded by a shell, killing his horse outright. I was quite close by the Major at the time; Several of our men were killed and wounded, but still we put our rifle fire into them. It was about six o'clock now when the Germans again opened upon us, their machine guns doing great execution but still we held them. About quarter past six the Germans made a great rush under cover of their guns, it was at this moment when a shell struck within 5 yards of us, covered us with dirt, but never exploded. Half past six they made another attack with their machine guns, and at this moment they swept the whole lot of us out, the butt of my rifle was split to pieces and I was wounded in both legs, twice in the left arm, and clean through the mouth which left me helpless on the ground with the loss of blood, and unable to move. Just getting dark and the Germans came through us and handled us very rough. Then a German officer spoke to me in good English and said 'You are a prisoner in our hands, I leave two soldiers here with you and send you back to hospital, where you will be treated and then sent to Germany.'
(*Private C Fussell*)

When we reached our new position things were quiet for a while until some Uhlans appeared on the skyline and a German aeroplane flew over us. Then things warmed up again. Shrapnel began to burst all round us making it too hot to stay. So we retired into the outskirts of Ligny and began to loophole the houses. That was no good, so we took up a position in an orchard, fixed bayonets and waited. In the meantime we had a good feed off the fruit trees. This was cut short by shrapnel coming from our front and flanks which made us evacuate the village already under heavy shellfire, especially the Church which was being used as a Red Cross hospital.
(*Arthur Cook*)

At about 4.30 p.m. General Smith Dorrien, having achieved his objective of regrouping II Corps decided to break off contact with the enemy. However verbal orders issued by 4th Division Headquarters did not reach all the units in the front line, leading to a fragmented withdrawal.

Shortly after 5.00 p.m. the remains of the Somersets retired from the battlefield under the cover of General Sordet's French corps, which had now arrived to relieve the British. The Battalion had become divided into two parties – one under Lieutenant-Colonel Swayne, who had with him the survivors of two companies, and the other under Major Prowse. Orders given to the Brigade had been to retire on Vendhuille by way of Malincourt and Aubencheul, and with this intention Colonel Swayne set out first – the remainder of the Battalion remaining in Ligny, in touch with the enemy until a late hour.

After a march of about 12 miles, Colonel Swayne with 8 officers and about 150 men reached Aubencheul that night, and billeted. The half Battalion under Major Prowse had, however, taken the road to Clary, where it met with troops belonging to the 3rd Division and so pushed on to Elincourt. Outside the latter village the party fell in with the G.O.C. and other units of the Brigade and subsequently spent the night at Serain.
(*History*)

About 4.30 p.m. we had an order to leave the village and we marched Prowse, Yatman, Jones-Mortimer, Ford, Holt and I and about 200 men. We were given the general direction of St. Quentin in which to retire. As we got a mile or two away from Ligny we heard the French at last coming up as we could hear the peculiar rattle of their guns and saw their shells bursting. There was a feeling of relief and we all hoped they were giving the Germans a bit of their own back. We continued our march, but were overtaken by the General and his Staff, who told us we were to billet at a little village called Malincourt for the night. This was welcome news, as it seemed that we could not be so hard pressed after all. We found rather scattered billets for our men about 9.00 p.m. and I got into a house with Ford and it was a great pleasure to sit down to a meal of coffee and fried eggs and also to get a wash. Ford and I got a bed, and actually took all our clothes off though we did not expect to get more than four hours sleep and in reality got considerably less.
(*W Whittuck*)

They had reached the top of a hill a little to the south of Ligny, pressed by the Germans who sent after the British a tremendous shower of shells which created great havoc. The ground was covered with killed and wounded men. Whilst making his way down the hill Lance Corporal Herbert Besley came across an artilleryman with a bad shell wound in the head. Despite the torrent of projectiles he picked him up, threw him across his shoulders and ran as fast as he could with his burden, his arms and the accoutrements on his back. He had not gone far when a shell came along exploded near him, blew his wounded comrade to pieces, carried away the corporal's knapsack, struck his cap from his head, forced his rifle from hand and hurt him severely in the back. A huge bruise more than an incised or punctured wound. So tremendous was the shock that the corporal became unconscious and knew nothing more until he found himself in the field hospital from whence he was ultimately transferred to Bristol Infirmary. The corporal asserts that possibly he would have been blown to pieces had he not on his shoulder the unconscious artilleryman who received the brunt of the shell explosion.

(*Somerset County Gazette*)

We had a French interpreter there and after we had been dressed he started to tell those wounded who could walk to go to the rear. On the way we caught up with three carts with 16 men and a medical orderly. The officer put me in charge of the carts and told me to take them to a station about six miles away. When we reached the station we found the lines occupied by the Germans so I went with the carts to the next station nine miles further on. The stationmaster tried to get a message through to St Quentin but all the wires were out. The French people who were driving their carts were just as anxious as we were to get of danger, so we drove on to another village eight or nine miles back and there we got to a French hospital. A Medical Officer saw to the dressings of the men, but four of them were so bad we had to leave them in the hospital.

(*Archibald Miles, Bath Chronicle*)

I shall never forget the scene as long as I shall live. The seriously wounded were left there. As I said before there were no ambulances near, so those of us who were wounded and could walk made our way to the place where the wounded were being attended to. We could not get our wounds dressed there so we went to another place but it was just the same. Eventually we came to the field ambulance at Caudry and the officer put us in a cart and sent us to Le Cateau to be put on the ambulance train. However we could not get any train so we went on to Bosigny, but still no luck. At the next village we came to we found a hospital and there a chum and I had our wounds dressed.

(*J. Tadd – Bath Chronicle*)

No supplies were issued to the Battalion on this day. At the conclusion of this action only some 8 officers and 150 men were collected under the C.O. Other parties however collected under Major Prowse and Lieutenant Montgomery respectively and ultimately rejoined the C.O.'s party. After the last formed body had rejoined the casualties were found to be 19 N.C.O.s and men known to be killed, 9 officers and 150 N.C.O.s and men known to be wounded (and some thought to be killed) and 100 N.C.O.s and men missing, of the latter many were killed or wounded. It is worth recording that the Battalion went into action at this battle without any stretchers, as the whole of the 1st line transport (less SAA carts) had been withdrawn from the Battalion the previous evening.

Chapter Three

Retreat to the Marne
27th August–5th September

27th August

German advanced guard passed through at 9.00 a.m. Gun and rifle fire but getting further and further away, which was not very encouraging. Found I was very stiff and the only thing I could move was my left leg. During the afternoon, two German officers came in formally and took over the hospital. They took all weapons, field glasses and maps but beyond that were fairly civil. A guard was put on the hospital and all equipment was collected and burnt (bang went about £30). We were fed and looked after by the women of the French Red Cross of the village and luckily had some of our own doctors to look after us. (*O Philby*)

On the morning of the 27th August, Private Long, also prisoner of 'B' Company of the 1st Battalion came to see me. He told me that our gallant officer Major Thoyts, our Company officer died of his wounds during the night of the 26th, in the next room to me, which I was sorry to hear.
(*C H Fussell*)

The headquarters party left their billets at 2.00 a.m. With no definite orders as where to proceed the Commanding Officer decided to move towards St Quentin. After marching south for some three miles the troops were fired upon by a sentry who did not challenge. The sentry was found to be British and the village Vendhuille, in which 4th Division Headquarters were resting. Colonel Swayne then rejoined the Division.

After collecting supplies, the Battalion, with main body of the 11th Brigade, marched to Bernes with a midday halt at Hesbercourt. At Bernes a defensive position was taken up and held until 7.00 p.m. The Germans did not press the pursuit and the Battalion did not come to action. At 9.00 p.m. the Battalion marched with the rest of the Division in a southerly direction. Civilian carts had been hired and men were given lifts in relays.

Pass through Roissel, but halt for food at small hamlet of Hervilly. Inhabitants are most kind and generous. Some of all four regiments in our Brigade are now together. Colonel Biddulph takes command, and is ordered to hold Bernes, which we do until about 7.00 p.m. Drunken Irishman creates momentary panic by galloping in on exhausted horse, shouting that he is being pursued by German Cavalry Corps. Division, at 9.00 p.m., commences 16 miles night march. Officers and men take turns to ride on gun-limbers, country carts and horses. This night march was carried out excellently by all concerned. Taking into consideration what the troops had undergone during the two previous days, they rose to the occasion in a wonderful fashion, proving again the enormous capacity for endurance which is possessed by the British soldier.

> During daylight the 4th Division had shown a bold front to the enemy in the dead of night it fell back, sullen but undismayed, maintaining its discipline
> (*W Watson*)

As it began to grow light we were taken off the roads and had to march across country, which was very trying as the weather was hot and. our feet were sore. Some men's feet already were in a shocking state. About 10.00 a.m. it was evident that we could not get any further without something to eat but though there were villages about and farms, they were all deserted and we were off the beaten track of any larger villages or towns. We eventually found a village where we managed to get the men a little bread, sardines and chocolate. We had just started our own meal and very good it looked too, when we heard guns firing and a message came that we were to get on the move at once again with the Hampshires as rearguard. Shells were bursting in the village now and it seemed very hard to have to leave it when we had only just told the pardrone who had fed us that the Germans would not come. The outposts had let a small party of German cavalry dressed as peasants into the village and they were making things very unpleasant. We left the village and then cut across country to some high ground to the south. It was now raining heavily and on the top of the hill we found one of our heavy guns stuck fast in the mud. My Company was ordered to lay on to the drag ropes and we eventually pulled it out, but the shells were falling pretty heavily, though as a matter of fact those who stuck to the gun were not touched, whilst those who scattered were almost all knocked out. We had some tremendously heavy plough fields to cross to the next ridge and I regret to say that some men threw away their equipment and rifles. As I arrived on the top of the next ridge with about 30 men I was asked by a Gunner Major to act as escort to a section of guns. I could not communicate with Yatman but managed to rally the men and extend behind some corn stacks where we had a good field of fire on to the ridge we had just evacuated. I held on here till the guns withdrew, but did not see anything of the enemy except a cavalry patrol, which quickly withdrew. I next

retired on to a road running parallel to the ridge, where chaos reigned as the 3rd Division were retiring along it whilst we wanted to cross it. I eventually crossed with a view to joining up with Yatman who had given the direction of retirement as a thickly wooded hill still further in rear. I had only just started to move on when I saw Jones-Mortimer with some men and joined up with him. We decided to join the 3rd Division and retire with them, as we had not an idea where to go having no maps. We joined up with Prowse and Yatman and still moved mostly across country, which was very trying for marching, as the mud caked on one's boots. We eventually got on to the road, still marching in a southerly direction, poor Yatman in a very footsore condition, as he had no horse. In fact Prowse alone had his horse. We continued marching on till we reached a village about 6.00 p.m. where of all luxuries we got a glass of beer each. We then moved on to another small village, having to take cover once or twice from aeroplanes on the way, where we halted in a large farm. We hoped we might stop there for the night but by 8.00 p.m. we were on the move again but with the welcome news that we were to be taken by wagon to St. Quentin. Boyd, our Brigade Major, had been wounded in the shoulder on the 26th, but had stuck it till this evening when he was luckily able to be transferred to an ambulance wagon. I gave him all my emergency tea ration. When we got to the main road to St. Quentin, there was a continual stream of transport and gun limbers passing and on to these we had to put the men. I got all my men on but had to walk myself until I got so tired that I got up on one of the leaders of a gun team. He was a quiet horse and I stopped there till I fell off fast asleep. I finished the rest on foot, though I had one or two falls on the way from being fast asleep. It was not a nice sensation.
(*W Whittuck*)

We were having breakfast in a village when their guns caught us unaware and gave us a hot time for a bit. I counted eight shells, which fell within anything from fifteen to forty yards of me. You hear the bang as the gun is fired, then you hear a sort of whistle gradually going up the scale and you can generally tell when its coming anywhere near you and if you are wise you lie down flat as muck and wait till the shell has exploded.
(*Edward Packe*)

28th August

The night march proved to be arduous through Vraignes and Tetry to Voyennes, which was reached about 6.00 a.m. after a march of about 12 miles. Here a party of 4 officers and about 300 other ranks under Major Prowse rejoined Headquarters. The Battalion was allotted billets but before they could be occupied the order was given to move as German cavalry was pressing in pursuit. No supplies were obtainable and the order was given by The Commander in Chief to burn kits and bury ammunition, if necessary, in order that men might be carried on the wagons if not fit to march. This was not, however, found to be necessary in the Battalion. The march was resumed at about 10.00 a.m. and short halts were made at Hombleux and Libremont. At the latter place (reached at 5.00 p.m.) bread and wine and apples were purchased locally. At 7.00 p.m. the Battalion marched to Campagne and was compelled to halt owing to a transport breakdown ahead. About five hours sleep were obtained by the roadside.

> Form column of route about 3.00 p.m. and march on Libremont, where General requisitions wine and bread for men. The Mayor gives Prowse, Sutton and myself a splendid meal – omelette, coffee, and fruits. "Vive la France." Continued march about 6 p.m., but only reach outskirts of Freniches. Sleep on side of road.
> (*W Watson*)

> Orders were then given that all our baggage (Officers) was to be destroyed. The Rifle brigade and Hampshires destroyed theirs, but luckily the East Lancs and our transport could not be found at the time. We continued marching all that day moving for the most part in artillery formation, but though we heard the guns distinctly, we did not see anything of the enemy.
> (*W Whittuck*)

> Retirement continued for about six miles, when we lined a bank for three hours, but nothing came of it. A rumour went round that German cavalry were coming through the village. This caused a commotion and men of other units in front panicked and rushed through our lines like mad-men, knocking over some of our men. We lined another bank and waited, but it was a false alarm, it being only French cavalry.
> The Brigade moved off again at 4.00 p.m. to a village where we had one and a half hours rest. Here wine and apples were given to us. Moved off again at 8.00 p.m., but owing to the danger of being ambushed we slept on the road-side during the night.
> We have not seen any of our transport for some time, which was under the command of Captain Prideaux. We are a very elusive battalion these days.
> (*Arthur Cook*)

29th August

At 5.00 a.m. the march was resumed and no pursuit was apparent. About 9.00 a.m. a halt was taken at Sermaize and breakfasts and dinners were eaten. During the afternoon Germans were reported close at hand and a further withdrawal became necessary. The Battalion marched at 8.00 p.m. and reached Sempigny at about 10.00 p.m. Here a few hours sleep were obtained in a field.

> Colonel Swayne informs Company Commanders that "Bunter" says situation is again critical, that it is on the cards we may be surrounded by superior

forces. Inglorious way to end one's first campaign. However, consoling thought – others in previous wars have been in worse plight and overcome their difficulties. (Keep this information from young officers and men, as moral effect might be bad.)
(*W Watson*)

Moved off at 3.00 a.m. doing about ten miles to Sermaize where we had food and wine and fresh supplies from our transport which has now turned up at last.

I saw my first aeroplane fight today between a German and a French. I could not see the finish of it but it was reported the German came to grief. On the march again at 7.30 p.m., doing about twelve miles before bivouacing in a clover field for a couple of hours, when the retirement was resumed.

Most of the men have discarded all their equipment except a bandolier or two of ammunition and their rifle. This would have meant severe disciplinary action in normal times, but nobody seems to mind as long as they keep their rifle and ammunition. I shall stick to the whole of my equipment in spite of being advised by others to get rid of it. Though the days are terrifically hot, the nights are very cold and I am glad of my greatcoat while the other are shivering. But it is hard work humping all this on my back, mile after mile, in blazing sunshine.
(*Arthur Cook*)

30th August

The march was resumed at 5.00 a.m. and at 6.00 a.m. Lieutenant Montgomery and a further party of about 300 N.C.O.s and men rejoined the Battalion. A halt of about 3 hours was made at Tracy le Mont and biscuits and cheese were issued. At about 2.00 p.m. the Battalion moved again. The weather was extremely hot. After a long and trying march of about 15 miles in great heat Pierrefonds was reached at about 10.00 p.m. The men were very tired and hungry, but were able to purchase bread and wine in the town. Owing to smallpox, billets were not available and the Battalion slept in the streets. A full issue of rations was made during the night.

From:	11th Brigade
To:	**Rifle Brigade, Hampshires, East Lancs, Somerset L.I**
Date:	**30th August**
Time:	**1430**

The march will be resumed at once to the original destination viz Troisly-Breuil. the battalions will join the line of march as they find it most convenient, As long as each battalion marches smartly and as a complete unit the G.O.C. Division will take the salute at a point on the road near Morneval Farm.

Map 3
Retreat August. *History of the Light Somerset Light Infantry 1914–18*

We reached Pierrefonds at midnight, after the worst march we had had. Going up a wooded hill at night and then having to go down again when we might have skirted it. The East Lancs were a bit mutinous. The men had to lie in the streets as there was scarlet fever in the village but there was an issue of rum. We had an excellent omelette.
(*W Whittuck*)

Staff work is bad. No guides to show us the way in the wood. No billets arranged in the town. Men sleep on straw in the streets. All very tired, but in good spirits. Have long talk at dinner with French Staff Officer, who takes a most optimistic view of our situation. Hope he may be right.
(*W Watson*)

We did about ten miles and then rested in a small town where we had some tea
– the first for four or five days. It went down a treat.

It is Sunday; the Church bells were ringing for morning service and civilians
wending their way to Church. It turned our thoughts to home and made us wish
we were going to our own churches. After three hours rest we were off again
and continued until 10.30 p.m – 6 1/2 hours! The heat was stifling during the day,
however, we stuck it mile after mile. God only knows, our throats are parched
with heat and dust and every ten minutes halt is spent in a sleep of exhaustion.
We are too far-gone to look or talk to anyone. We are moving as if in a dream
and no one knows where we are going. Every now and again a man drops down
and we help him up and try to urge him on. Others fall out by the roadside too
exhausted to go another step. No one takes any notice. Perhaps they will die, or
be made prisoner. Our feet are red raw with blisters, our limbs numbed for want
of rest, all interest in things has gone, but we keep going, how we do not know.
Some of us try to keep disciplined formation, but it is hopeless. There are no
signs of any sections' of fours. We are hobbling along in one rabble. Officers and
senior N.C.O.s try to set an example by sticking to their men, but there is no
"Get up in line," or "Left, right, left." Refugees are mixed up with us, old men
and women, with their sole belongings in an old pram, or trolley, or else on their
backs. It is pitiful to see them, especially a young mother with a child in arms
and a couple of tots hanging onto her skirts. Sometimes a Tommy will help her
along, or carry the child, when it is as much as he can do to keep going himself.
We halted for the night at Pierrefonds, but owing to rumours of smallpox, slept
in the roadway. We got a tot of rum and got down to sleep at 11.00 p.m. In spite
of our hard bed we slept like tops. (*Arthur Cook*)

31st August

A very hot day. The march was resumed at 7.00 a.m. through the Forest of
Compeigne which afforded welcome shade from the scorching sun. Billets were
allotted at Santines (15 miles), but just as they were to be occupied a report was
received of a large German force moving from Compeigne, and a defensive position
was taken up on high ground south of St Sauveur. No attack was made during the
night and the men got a much-needed sleep. A full days rations were issued tonight

> We rested at Pierrefonds but were early on the move again reaching St.
> Sauveur Courcelle when we were told that there was a German Corps march-
> ing diagonally to meet us and it was not thought that we could get clear before
> they came up with us. We remained in a little wood just outside the village
> most of the day, the Hampshires and East Lancs being sent out as outposts.
> We had orders to get as much rest as possible and that we should probably
> remain there the night, as transport and guns were not yet clear of the road. I
> was just settling off to sleep when I was ordered to move out with two sections
> in the direction of Bethissy as a picket, to watch some ground the Hampshires

could not guard. I was rather annoyed at the idea, as I had had toothache, having broken another tooth. I knew that in the dark I should not be able to get in touch with anyone on my right or left. I reached a little farm where I posted my sentry groups to watch both the road to Bethissy and a track leading to some high ground which the East Lancs were occupying. With the remainder of my men I lay down on some straw and got some sleep.

(*W Whittuck*)

Roused at 5.00 a.m., had a good breakfast and were given two days rations. Today we are escorting guns and transport. We stopped in a town for an hour, just when Brigadier Hunter-Weston arrived. He complimented us on our wonderful bearing and marching and said, "I cannot make your Regiment out, for no matter how tired you are you are always so cheerful." The march went on until 1.00 p.m., in terrific heat and many men collapsed in dead faints. During the last two days we have been marching through the Forest of Compeigne. It was cool under the trees by day, but very close and muggy at night. On our midday halts food was ready for us including barrels of French beer. Nothing was arranged for teetotalers like myself to drink. I stuck it out for several days in spite of the size of my thirst. I sat and watched the boys as they filled up their mess tins with beer and came back to drink it, all frothy, in front of me, pulling my leg. Today it was especially hot and my resistance weakened. When the order came to fall in with mess tins, I was in the queue like a shot and came back with my tin full and running over. I thought to myself, "If I get intoxicated the boys will help me along." Down it went, all honey sweet and I smacked my lips. To my astonishment I felt no ill effects and could walk in a straight line. I shall be in the beer queue every day in future. We went on all that afternoon and evening reaching a village about 1.30 a.m. and had a short sleep. Several lots of firing during the night but we were not disturbed.

(*Arthur Cook*)

1st September

Marched at 7.00 a.m. with orders to occupy a rearguard position. The Hants and East Lancs were disposed on high ground north of St Saveur and Vaucelles. The Somerset Light Infantry and Rifle Brigade in a ridge north of Santines and Verberie. The Somerset L.I. were disposed 'D' Company on the right of the Hants, Battalion H.Q., 'A', 'B' and 'C' Companies and Machine Gun section on the ridge north of Santines holding la Haute Berme Farm. 'D' Company were soon heavily engaged. The Hants and East Lancs suffered somewhat heavily and retired about 8.30 a.m. The opposition consisted of cavalry and horse artillery. 'D' Company covered the Hants retirement and themselves retired about 9.00 a.m. on the main position. The Germans appeared to have suffered heavily and did not press the pursuit, and about 10.00 a.m. the Battalion formed up in Artillery formation and moved across a wide-open plain towards Ruilly. Here the Battalion formed up and rested, and about 3.00

p.m. moved to Rozieres, which was reached at 6.00 p.m. Total distance marched about 10 miles. The battalion suffered four casualties, 1 man from 'A' Company was left for dead. Rozieres was occupied by the Germans during the day. The Battalion billeted in a large farm. Supplies were issued during the night.

> About 2.00 a.m. there was some sharp rifle fire in the village I had just left and a gun was also fired. In the morning I discovered all this noise had been made by three Uhlans who somehow had broken through the line and were supposed to have come back along our road, but I only saw a party of French Cuirassiers just as it was getting light. I hoped that we might get some breakfast, but it never arrived, then the remainder of my Company came up at about 7.00 a.m. I had heard from villagers that the Germans were actually in Bethissy which was only about a mile further on. There was certainly very heavy gunfire there in the morning and it turned out afterwards to be the fight of 'L' Battery R.H.A. and our cavalry surprised in the mist by German guns at close range. I remained where I was, keeping touch with Yatman, and the remainder of the Company who had occupied the high ground to the right of the East Lancs. About 11.00 a.m, we had orders to retire and Yatman and the Hampshires fell back on me. As they passed me and got on to the road St. Sauveur Courcelle, fire was opened from a wood quite close to us. The Hampshires sent out a patrol to discover who was firing at us, but now rifle fire seemed to be coming from the direction in which we had to retire, so we thought we were in rather a bad way. Eventually we retired to a stream to the left of St. Sauveur Courcelle doubling across the open ground by sections. We lost no men. We did not discover who had fired at us till we reached some high ground above St. Sauveur Courcelle, where we found the Rifle Brigade who said they had been firing across the valley at about 50 Uhlans who had been firing at us, so that accounted for the shots coming from the direction in which we were to retire. We formed up with the rest of the battalion and marched across country in the direction of Rosiere which we reached after a very trying march about 7.00 p.m., On the way Prowse captured a Uhlan's horse at a little village we passed. Poor brute, it looked half starved and dead tired. We could see by this, however, that they were in front of us and on our flanks. We received a nasty shock too at Rosiere when we were told that about 400 German cavalry had passed through that day. However, we found the garden at the only chateau there well stocked and were preparing some sort of meal when Prideaux arrived with the transport, and rations were issued. He had had rather an exciting time on nearing the village as he had seen what he thought to be a patrol of our cavalry just off the road and had cantered up to ask the way. He was received with a very guttural tone and was chased up to our outposts.
>
> (*W Whittuck*)

Roused at 4.00 a.m. and had breakfast. A lot of artillery and rifle fire going on and we moved to take up a position on a very high hill. My platoon was overlooking flat ground and bushy hills. It was very misty and we could not see far.

We stayed here about an hour sniping at Uhlans who were cantering about

in threes and fours. Soon a gun on our left fired two shells which pitched on our right, well out of danger. All was quiet for fifteen minutes when a salvo of five fell again to our right. Then a gun in a wood opposite us began firing straight at us. The shells just skimmed the bank we were lining and burst directly behind us. We then picked up our rifles and retired, as this was a little too close to be pleasant. A shell passed clean through one of our men as we retired, killing him instantly. Luckily for us Jerry stopped firing. We retired for eight or nine miles and bivouaced in a farm. But there was no rest for my platoon, for we were detailed for outpost duty for the night.
(*Arthur Cook*)

2nd September

Marched at 2.00 a.m via Baron under peace conditions. Very Hot. Midday halt at Eve, billeted in a small and dirty farm. At 6.00 pm three companies were dispatched to Othis as part of scheme of defence of the neighbourhood. The Hants, East Lancs and Rifle Brigade were also disposed around Eve. At 9.00 p.m. guns and transport were sent off by themselves with Lagny as their destination. The Brigade followed at 10.00 p.m. 'B', 'C' and 'D' companies rejoined the Battalion just south of Dammartin at which place 11/3 hour's sleep was obtained.

'C' Company is advance guard to Brigade. A suspicious looking wood across our front. Brigadier pleased with dispositions. Long halt at Eve. Weather very hot and trying. At 4.00 p.m. three Companies on outposts covering this. My Company has an ideal night outpost line in low ground with dark background, facing rising ground and setting sun. We indeed can see without being seen. Orders to close, at 9.00 p.m. on Damartin.
(*W Watson*)

We had a fair night's rest, though I woke with a splitting headache, having had one very small glass of the padrone's champagne. We marched all day and most of the night.
(*W Whittuck*)

On the move at 2.00 a.m. but by 10.00 a.m. the heat was so intense that the march was stopped and we were put in a shed to cool off. The heat was stifling and good drinking water hard to obtain. We had a good supply of rations issued here. We passed through Baron this morning and are making our way towards Paris, about 28 miles away.

I and six men placed on outpost duty again tonight, but we had sudden orders to rejoin the battalion, which had already fallen in, and marched off at 11.45 p.m.
(*Arthur Cook*)

Halted for three hours in a farmyard and almost before you could turn round, I, and eight of my friends had a chicken, a pigeon and a rabbit, with spud, onions and carrots stewing away over a fire. It did make a good stew too. Clean up and doss down. Woken up to go on guard at Headquarters. Fall in again at 12.30 a.m. (*Edward Packe*)

3rd September

The march was then continued at 2.00 a.m. via Clay-Souilly and Lagny. Weather very hot and men distressed after ascending hill southeast of Lagny. Camp was still two miles ahead, so G.O.C. ordered Battalion to bivouac in any convenient chateau. Today's supplies issued about 8.00 p.m. There was a good supply of apples and bread to be obtained locally on which the Battalion subsisted. First mail from England arrived today. Ordered to move in evening to join rest of Brigade at their camp, but the order was cancelled at our request. Good rest today. Baggage wagons came up.

> We finished up two miles south of Lagny at 11.45 am. That was 12 hours continuous marching and the heat and dust were cruel, almost unbearable. We are feeling the effects of all this marching, but our platoon officer, Lieutenant Pretyman is smiling. He found a stray horse and goes along in front of us stretched out on the horse's back, fast asleep. We expect to see him fall off at any moment, but he doesn't! Today's march was roughly 28 miles over roads inches thick in dust. We look like a lot of millers, our clothes, faces and hands covered in dust, our mouths horribly parched. Everyone has a beard and with no washing facilities we look a set of horrors. Our numbers are gradually declining with men falling out each day. Being so near Paris we expect to see some kind of defence line set up, but it looks as if the French are going to surrender without a fight. Just before Lagny we saw some French lines with good trenches and further on some French gunners putting siege guns into position. But I doubt if they will be ready in time, as the enemy is close on our heels. We halted at 4.30 p.m. for tea. All the villages and towns we have passed through are being evacuated and crowds of refugees are fleeing.
> (*Arthur Cook*)

4th September

Moved at 6.15 a.m. to rejoin remainder of Brigade at Chateau de Fontanelle. Excellent bivouac in the shade and plenty of water, two miles from last night's bivouac. Were told we were to be here for two days to refit, but about 2.00 p.m. got orders to move at 4.00 p.m to Couvvray, which reached at 7.15 p.m. (about 6 miles). Seemed a good bivouac. Supplies were issued here. Again told we were to be here for two days and got orders about entrenching a position tomorrow, in the line of the Paris defences.

We reached Couvray the next day and moved on through the Pont de
Compiegne having an excellent dejeuner at a farm belonging to Emile de
Rothschild. The chateau was a most wonderful place with beautiful grounds.
It takes some enormous sum to keep up and is very rarely used by the family.
We managed to buy cigarettes, chocolate and matches for the men. This was
the first time I realized how much the men liked chocolate.

(*W Whittuck*)

5th September

Orders to move south at once as Germans had crossed the Marne, though apparently not in our vicinity. Marched at 2.00 a.m. via Serris, Jossigny, La Ferriere with
destination given as Chevry. Very hot march. Billets were allocated at Chevry but the
G.O.C. halted the Somerset L.I. and East Lancs at the Chateau de la Mausdaire two
miles short of Chevry and the Battalion bivouaced in the woods. Arrived about

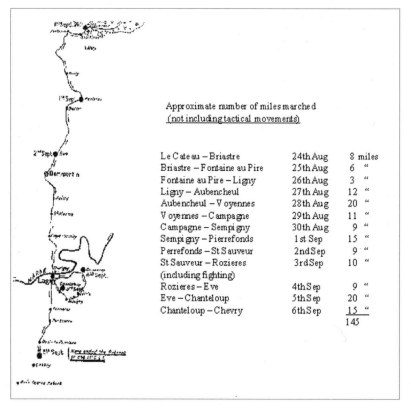

Approximate number of miles marched
(not including tactical movements)

Le Cateau – Briastre	24th Aug	8 miles
Briastre – Fontaine au Pire	25th Aug	6 "
Fontaine au Pire – Ligny	26th Aug	3 "
Ligny – Aubencheul	27th Aug	12 "
Aubencheul – Voyennes	28th Aug	20 "
Voyennes – Campagne	29th Aug	11 "
Campagne – Sempigny	30th Aug	9 "
Sempigny – Pierrefonds	1st Sep	15 "
Perrefonds – St Sauveur	2nd Sep	9 "
St Sauveur – Rozieres	3rd Sep	10 "
(including fighting)		
Rozieres – Eve	4th Sep	9 "
Eve – Chanteloup	5th Sep	20 "
Chanteloup – Chevry	6th Sep	15 "
		145

Map 4
Retreat September. *History of Somerset Light infantry 1914–18*

12 noon, marched about fifteen miles. On the way a two-hour breakfast halt was taken at La Ferriere and an excellent breakfast was provided for the officers by Baron Rothschild. Bread, chocolates, cigarettes and matches were purchased locally for the men. Supplies issued tonight. First reinforcements arrived, 90 men under 2nd Lieutenant Read.

Good news at last, British Army is to turn and advance. It appears German higher command has blundered. Joffre seizes his chance and slips a Corps or so between the Prussians, thus isolating their right army.

Our retreat is ended, perhaps worthy to be recorded in history by the side of Moore's to Corunna and Wellington's from Burgos, but we must have a Napier to tell the tale and do us justice. Lack of sleep has made me very irritable. No disorganization nor lack of discipline made its appearance in the 4th Division. The men bore their hardships and fatigue of the long night marches with dogged pluck, maintaining the highest traditions of the old 13th.

George and Charles were wonderful, always cheerful and never sparing themselves day or night. Charles is only 19, and joined last April. I can never repay the debt I owe to these two gallant boys.

(*W Watson*)

During this time our first reinforcement arrived after a day's march of about 40 miles. Read brought them up and they looked almost as footsore as we were, as they had been following us about practically the whole time since we had been in the country. We all thought that we should yet find ourselves in Paris, but the last thing we heard before we started to advance again from a point about 10 miles northeast of Paris was that we might have to retire into the South of France leaving Paris to the Germans. We had crossed the Aisne and the Marne where bridges were blown up but we never actually seemed to outdistance the enemy. Holt and Pretyman had to go sick during this period. We saw our valises once again but had to pack them up hurriedly and not being able to find my servant in a wood, I had to carry mine about 300 yards to the wagon. I vowed I would not be so keen about seeing it in future.

(*W Whittuck*)

At 1.00 a.m. was ordered to tell my Colour Sergeant (Pinky Paul) that the Battalion was moving at 3.45 a.m. At that hour we moved off and continued marching up to 2.00 p.m. when we were given two hours halt owing to the intense heat.

Our progress is very slow, about one mile an hour. Where is all this marching going to bring us to? Are we human beings or machines? During the march today a French aeroplane flew over us very low. The pilot waved his hand to us, which we cheerfully acknowledged.

(*Arthur Cook*)

Chapter Four

Advance to Aisne
6th–14th September

6th September

The retirement is over. Last night orders came that General French intended to take the offensive, having drawn the Germans down sufficiently far south. Marched about 7.00 a.m. to Jossigny (about 8 miles) where had a long halt, very hot. Our Brigade is acting as rearguard to whole British Army. It appears that 1st and 2nd Corps are scheduled to our right front and a French Army on our left and there are great hopes of heading off a German Corps before they can get across the Marne.

About 4.00 p.m. bivouaced in an apple orchard at Villeneuve de Comte, expecting to push on rapidly during night. Supplies issued during night at about 2.00 a.m.

> We have just heard that the Germans have been split and are retiring hard. Our 4th Division and 6th Division and the French are pursuing and we hope to cut them up all together. It is frightfully hot and very tiring walking. We are glad to be on the advance again.
> (F S Bradshaw)

> Good news today. THE RETREAT IS ENDED, but not our marching, for now we must turn round and chase Jerry for a change. He is in headlong flight and although we chased him for 15 or 16 miles we could not catch up with him, so bivouaced in a field near a farm, where we bought fresh milk for our tea. We got down to sleep at 8.30 p.m.
> (Arthur Cook)

7th September

Warned to move at 5.00 a.m., so breakfasted at 4.00 a.m. However got no definite order to march until 10.50 a.m when we were ordered to march at 10.40! Pity we breakfasted so early. Very hot day. The delay in starting appeared to have been caused a failure to get in touch with the French Corps on our left. Fear it may give Germans time to get away across the Marne. Pushed on slowly via Crecy to Maisoncelles, about 10 miles.

A comfortable bivouac was selected south of the village, but as we were about to occupy it, alarming news of German cavalry and motor machine guns being in the vicinity was brought in, so all battalions of the Brigade were disposed in fighting formation round the village. Settled down about 7.00 p.m. No alarms during night. Lieutenant Pretyman went sick today with dysentery.

> Sir John French's Special Order of the Day, in which the British Commander-in-Chief said: "I call upon the British Army in France to now show the enemy its powers, and to push on vigorously to the attack beside the Sixth French Army," was circulated to all units and read out to the men.
> (*History*)

> Enemy's machine gun batteries are reported to be hanging about to affect a surprise. Charles blocks road through hamlet with wagons, etc. Sleep well behind haystack just in rear of centre of my line. George and I ransack small chateau for food. Everything is just as the owner left it; his hat, coat and sticks, etc., are in the hall, rooms full of clothes, crockery and glass. The emptiness has an eerie effect on us both, and we are glad to get out into the open.
> (*W Watson*)

> Last night we had a very good omelette and some wine at The Hermitage and we had a very good breakfast at the same place. This is the best night that we have had so far, no scares or rapid orders to quit. Hear heavy firing again so expect we will be off soon. We did not move until 11.30 a.m. and then we marched in rather a muddle with R.E. and R.F.A. until 5.00 p.m. when we went into bivouac. The whole of the expeditionary force seems to be around here.
> (*F S Bradshaw*)

> Roused at 6.00 a.m. after the longest rest we have had since we have been in France. Marched at 11.00 a.m, and did ten miles in the full heat of the day. Our progress is very slow owing to so much transport on the road and the cruel heat. We could hardly see each other for the clouds of dust. It hovered round us like a fog and our throats are full of it. We had just finished marching at 5.30 p.m. when a report came that Jerry was having tea in a village just to our left. He did not stop to entertain us.
> (*Arthur Cook*)

8th September

Marched at 7.00 a.m and had slow and hot march to just south of Signey Signets (about 3 miles south of the Marne). Here found the advance guard of the 19th Brigade was held up by Germans north of the Marne. They had been badly caught by shellfire in column of ranks on the road. The 11th Brigade was diverted from the road and moved across country on the east side of the road, behind the artillery, which was heavily engaged, and eventually billeted just south of the river. 10th and 12th Brigades, during the night, gained ground on south bank of the Marne. The Battalion billeted in Chateau de Ventuille about 7.00 p.m. Rain fell heavily about 4.00 p.m, but the night was fine.

> It is now 6.30 a.m. and the first gun has gone off. Can't see how the Germans can escape, they must be cut off. They only got away from here half an hour before we got in. We are due to move east today with French on our right and left. A lot of German dead were found close to here yesterday.
>
> No good, we have let them go, and they have plumped some shells right into our advanced guard. Germans fire hell of a lot but don't seem to have done much good.
>
> (*F S Bradshaw*)

> Nine men attached to the 1st Battalion, Somerset Light Infantry having been on active service in France reported themselves at the Taunton Depot. The party, including two lance corporals and seven privates said they had been sent to Taunton from Folkestone where they had landed from one of the ports in France. The Somersets, with the rest of the British, experienced a trying time being outnumbered ten to one. When interviewed at the Depot the men told practically the same story, how during the constant retirements they had become separated from their companies and in perpetual dread of falling into the hands of the enemy. They wandered for days without food until they arrived at the coast. The men were all thankful to have come through the ordeal safely and regarded their escape as little short of miraculous.
>
> (*Somerset County Gazette*)

9th September

The 11th Brigade moved at 4.00 a.m and the advance towards the Marne began. The Brigade (after an officer's reconnaissance) followed a steep track leading northeast over the Petit Morin, at St. Martin. Order of March: Rifle Brigade, Somerset Light Infantry, East Lancs, and Hants. Had to move through thick woods down steep hill, which took some time. Rifle Brigade and Somerset L.I. got up to a position held by 12th Brigade on a ridge northeast of La Ferte under cover of darkness. Then took up position of observation at Les Abymes which was reached about 7.00 a.m. Spent whole day here, not under fire.

German snipers were posted in houses and buildings guarding the broken bridges over the Marne and the latter for a while were unapproachable. East Lancs ordered to clear the village. In doing this they lost their Colonel and about

40 men from the snipers. A little later the East Lancs again advanced to clear the enemy from the area around the bridge. 'C' Company ordered to support this attack with fire. In doing this came under heavy fire and lost one killed and three wounded. The enemy, however, did not stay to meet the attack by the East Lancs but retired up the slope of the hill north of La Ferte. 'C' Company and Machine Gun Section did some damage at long range, about 2000 yards, to the retiring Germans. About 6.00 p.m it was thought all Germans had retired from La Ferte. Battalion bivouaced in Chateau grounds at Les Abymes. Supplies issued about 2.00 a.m. 2nd reinforcement under 2nd Lieutenant Bush (90 men) arrived today.

When darkness fell on the 9th September only six battalions of the III Corps had crossed the Marne and of these three belonged to the 11th Infantry Brigade, i.e. Rifle Brigade, East Lancs and Hants; the 1st Somersets still remained just south of La Ferte. At 4.00 p.m. the Royal Engineers had begun work on the crossings over the Marne at La Ferte and when dawn broke on the following morning a pontoon and barrel bridge had been thrown across the river.
 (*History*)

On going forward to select suitable position, suddenly come under accurate rifle and machine-gun fire. Several men hit. Get a bullet through my haversack and riding breeches. Lie close here for short time. George with his platoon pushes on, on our left, and gets into some cottages. Believe our advance had good effect. Germans were seen withdrawing hastily and must have had a bad time from our guns, which made excellent shooting, plastering all their lines of retreat with shells.
(*W Watson*)

We were early on the move and crossed a small stream and then up onto a ridge overlooking the Marne. A glorious morning after a very hot night. We heard machine gun fire and it was evident that the further bank of the river was held by the Germans and there were certainly small parties on our side. I had to go forward to reconnoitre a way through a wood on the outskirts of La Ecole to find a position for 'B' and my Companies, whose job was to engage the enemy whilst the remainder of the Brigade crossed the river further east. I got to the edge of the wood overlooking the river and though I saw nothing, I had a few bullets whizzing round me directly I exposed myself. I went back and reported to the Colonel and led the two Companies down to what proved to be a good position. Though the enemy were not often visible we undoubtedly did good by continually worrying them with long-range fire. We reported an excellent target of an enemy's convoy to the artillery but owing to some misjudgment they failed to come up in time.
 (*W Whittuck*)

My platoon was ordered to go back a little as bodyguard to the General and his

Staff. We had been there about 30 minutes when a machine gun started firing at us. Luckily there was a good ditch and wall between us and the gunner, or we might have had casualties. It came as a surprise as we thought this area was clear. The guns were soon on to them and made them hop out of it. We moved up shortly after this to join the Battalion and were told to cook our breakfast. There is a rattle of musketry in the air this morning and after breakfast I had to take some men out to watch a road which was under long range fire from a machine gun. A few spent bullets fell around us causing no damage. Volunteers were called for to bury the dead. I and 24 others volunteered. We were given picks and shovels and marched about one and a half miles, but on arrival found we were not wanted, so we sat down on a lawn for a bit of a rest before rejoining the Battalion.

(*Arthur Cook*)

Private Nash, ex Bristol City footballer, recalls his first fight whilst the Somersets were sitting by the roadside preparing a meal from apples and pears from a neighbouring orchard. The news came that the German rearguard were fortifying the village and after the artillery wrought destruction on the houses, the Somersets were ordered to charge. The village lay at the foot of a slope and as the Somersets charged down them the Germans fired machine guns from the windows of the houses. Amidst the rain of shot Lieutenant Parr, son of the late Major General Sir Henry Hallam Parr of Wincanton, led his section on, nonchalantly remarking to Nash that it was 'a bit hot'. The Somersets could not be stopped and the Germans did not stop to meet them at close quarters.

Everywhere the inhabitants welcomed them with open arms, giving them food, fruit in hampers, red wine and tobacco. But so precious and scarce was the English variety of the last mentioned that one man gave sixpence for not more than a third of one cigarette.

(*E Nash, Somerset County Gazette*)

10th September

Marched at 5.15 a.m with orders to cross the Marne by the pontoon bridge, which Royal Engineers had built during night. East Lancs and Hants had crossed in boats overnight. On reaching La Ferte about 6.00 a.m, Battalion was ordered to furnish fatigue parties and not cross till whole Division had crossed. The Battalion rested in a grindstone factory in La Ferte where bread, matches, chocolate and tobacco obtained by purchase. Got over bridge at 1.00 p.m. and soon caught up remainder of Brigade. 'A' Company was left at La Ferte to defend bridge. Battalion went into comfortable billets at Chalon at about 6.00 p.m. Marched about 10 miles. Inhabitants delighted to see British troops as Germans had been in village for a week and had used up all the supplies. General Snow, Commander 4th Division, injured today by fall from his horse. General Wilson took command of Division.

I remained on as orderly officer in case any messages had to be taken to the Battalion during the night. As so often happened I was not told when the Battalion had orders to move and so was greeted rather irately by the Colonel in the morning when he rode up to Brigade Headquarters and found me trying to get some breakfast. The Battalion was on in front. We halted on the southern bank of the Marne in an old mill yard, where we had a good breakfast and shave. The Hampshires had crossed by night in boats whilst the Engineers had erected an excellent pontoon bridge close to where the old bridge had been blown up by the Germans. It was now evident to us that the Germans had got well away and that the stubborn resistance made to our crossing the previous day had all been due to machine guns mounted on motor cars and cyclists. One could not help admiring their pluck as our guns had bombarded the town heavily when once they had got over their scruples of firing at apparently unoccupied houses. We crossed the Marne about noon having accomplished this in about 36 hours, when we afterwards discovered from prisoners that the Germans had hoped to hold us up here for about four days. It was very hot and I think the stench in the town was the worst I experienced during the time I was out there. Our ambulance men were already busy burying Germans, but the road had many carcasses of horses by its side.
(*W Whittuck*)

As soon as I was awake I saw men dashing about with loaves of bread and made hurried enquiries as to where it came from. I was soon back with eight loaves, a rare armful, as each loaf was about 3 feet long. Bread is eagerly sought after when available. All the bridges round La Ferte are blown up and the Royal Engineers have succeeded in erecting a pontoon over the river. Our platoon was told to help traffic up the riverbank after crossing the pontoon.

We started this work at 7.30 a.m. and were relieved at 10.30 a.m. for a rest, for it was hard work pushing vehicles up the slope. It is very stormy today, but we get a fair amount of shelter under the destroyed bridges when not helping traffic. A 1.00 p.m. a lot of French Lancers crossed the pontoon, they looked very business-like. Corporal Still and six men of my section went to the hospital and brought three prisoners back. The Battalion crossed the pontoon at 1.00 p.m., taking the prisoners and also two men in civilian clothes. 'A' Company is left behind as bridge guard. Later, four prisoners of German 66th Regiment were handed over to us, with 20 German rifles and ammunition. We broke up the rifles and threw them with the ammunition into the river. Our platoon can say that it pushed and shoved the B.E.F. on its way to chase Jerry! After a good supper we got down to sleep by the bridge about 9.00 p.m.
(*Arthur Cook*)

11th September

Marched at 4.15 a.m. at short notice, which might have been avoided by better

Brigade Staff work. Cloudy and chilly morning. East Lancs and Rifle Brigade have billeted farther head. We joined rest of Brigade at Vendrest and the march was resumed via Coulombs and Hervillers Found a French Brigade on our road and had to wait for them to pass. Stayed at St Quentin for about two hours to allow 5th Division to pass. Started about 3.00 p.m. to march to Passy to billet. Rained heavily when we started and continued to about 7.00 p.m. Battalion billeted at a farm at 6.00 p.m. Men in barns, officers in billiard room of chateau. Lit large fires and soon all got dry. Marched about 12 miles. Peaceful night. No supplies were issued that night, the supply-wagons not turning up. Germans seem to have got clean away and our visions of getting round them have vanished. The delay on the 7th must have done the harm.

All the roads were very congested with French and English troops. The road was littered with German dead horses, broken motors, bicycles, and two aeroplanes. The road was ankle deep in mud. We passed a German supply depot, containing big gun ammunition, flour and rice – the bags of the two latter articles had W.D. Aldershot on them. There was also a captured French aeroplane riddled with shrapnel bullets.
(*G Prideaux*)

Sappers started dismantling bridge at 4.00 a.m. Bridge cleared at 6.00 a.m. Had very good breakfast. Had good bathe yesterday in the Marne. Left about 9.00 a.m., began to rain 2.00 p.m., got very wet. Had half an hour for lunch then Colonel Jones, Royal Engineers, wanted to get on so we pushed off and got all mixed up amongst the Train. At 6.00 p.m. we were fed up and turned into a large farm where there was nothing to eat, but plenty of straw and it was warm. Met a Padre who had been badly treated by the Germans, who had taken him prisoner. Don't know where the R.E. are whom we are supposed to be escorting. We have three German prisoners.
(*F Bradshaw*)

Roused at 4.00 a.m. by R.E. wagons coming alongside us to pick up the bridge. We set to and helped them. This over we had breakfast and marched at 9.00 a.m. and continued slogging along up to 5.30 p.m. It seems that Jerry can run faster than we can. We covered about 16 miles, the latter half being in pouring rain.
(*Arthur Cook*)

12th September

Lieutenant Colonel Swayne received a note conveyed by a Medical Officer during the night from General Hunter-Weston advising him to go home on sick leave. He had been very run down lately. He decided to take advantage of the opportunity and went off in the supply wagon this morning. Major Prowse taking over command of the Battalion.

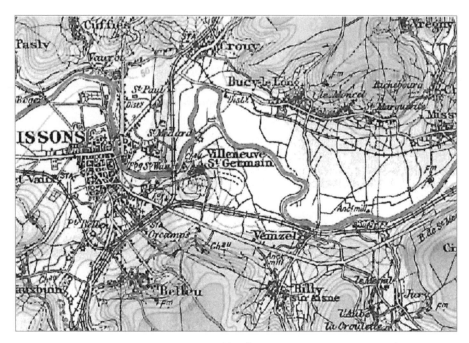

Map 5
Aisne Area. (*Official History CD Rom Naval and Military Press*)

Owing to the temporary detention of the supply wagon by O.C. 'A' Company last night, no supplies arrived during the night. A quarter ration, carried on the cook's cart was given to the men and eaten by them for breakfast at 2.15 a.m, as a preliminary order to move at 3.30 a.m had been received. However no move was made until 7.00 a.m. Marched through beautiful country and had midday halt at Montramboeuf Farm, but there was nothing to eat and so the men went hungry again. Germans appeared to be holding a ridge about three miles north of this and Divisional H.Q. ordered the Battalion to deploy for action, but did not advance to attack. We waited for some three hours in artillery formations in a cold wind then reformed column of route and moved about 5.00 p.m towards Septmonts About 6.00 p.m it started raining and continued very heavily for the rest of the night.

> Germans were evidently close in front of us as the inhabitants informed us that they had only passed through in the morning. It came on to pour with rain in the afternoon and we got soaked to the skin. A Brigade of Scotsmen passed us on the march. I hope we did not look quite as bad as they did, mostly limping, unshaven and many without caps or equipment and in one or two cases without rifles. They had had a very hard time.
> (*W Whittuck*)

Left St Quentin at 7.00 a.m. and began a fatiguing march to Villentoire, amongst the wagons all day, and raining most of the time. Pulled up at a good farm at 6.30 p.m. and thought we should have it to ourselves but during the night R.F.A., R.A.M.C., and A.S.C. began crowding in. Saw Prideaux who says the battalion has no food. Very heavy firing all day. We expect to hear the Germans have given in very soon.

(*F Bradshaw*)

13th September

Started off in pouring rain and with empty stomachs. Reached Veneziel (7 miles) about 1.00 a.m and waited for about an hour to get across bridge. Men very tired and hungry. Crossed in single file about 2.00 p.m and formed up on north bank. Then marched in column of route across plain to Bucy le Long, arriving there just at daylight (about 4.15 a.m). There was no information about the Germans except that from the appearance of the houses they must have made a hurried exit as a result of our shellfire the previous evening. The Brigade seized the ridges north of the village, Rifle Brigade on the right, Hants in the centre, Somerset L.I on left, East Lancs in reserve. The summit about 300 feet was reached without opposition: but moving across the plateau on top of the ridge German cavalry was to be seen at a range of about 800 yards. German infantry were in trenches and also a tool cart. In fact the ridge appeared to be strongly held. It seems incomprehensible that the passage across the bridge or the open plain between the river and village or still more the narrow paths up the hill should not have been held by the Germans. It can only be assumed that they did not anticipate any British advance on such a wild night and after the long march the troops had already had. The total distance marched by the Battalion since 7.00 a.m yesterday was 25 miles, including 2 deployments for attack, mostly in pouring rain and no food since 12.15 a.m on the 12th. Fortunately the day was warm and the men were able to get some sleep and bread and vegetables were requisitioned and a good meal provided. During the day the Battalion was heavily shelled but no loss was suffered.

On the morning of September 13th Sir John French gave orders that his force was to advance and make good the Aisne.

In anticipation of much-needed rest the Somerset L.I. had gone into billets in Septmonts at 8.00 p.m. on 12th, but the Battalion had barely settled down, when about 10.00 p.m. the men were ordered to turn out and form up ready to march off at 7.00 p.m. 11th Brigade Headquarters had received orders that after halting to get food (non-productive in the case of the Somersets) it was to push on and, if possible, seize the crossings over the Aisne at Venizel, a few miles east of Soissons. At Venizel, the Aisne runs in a flat valley from two to three miles wide, with steep hills on its northern bank. The slopes and crests are wooded, the tops or summits bare, but cultivated, rather similar to a monk's shaven crown with a ring of hair round the base of the skull. While the Brigade halted in Septmonts two officers, accompanied by a local guide, went forward to reconnoitre the route. Having finished their reconnaissance these officer's orders were, the senior officer was to remain in observation on the bridge and, if possible, find out whether the enemy was holding the opposite bank, whilst the junior officer returned to guide the column. The very severe physical strain which the reconnaissance entailed was too much for the junior officer, who, on returning (the 11th Brigade Diary records) was completely exhausted and incapable either of movement or of coherent speech. He had unfortunately dismissed the local guide and the column was thus forced to move forward by map direction.

After a march of seven miles the Battalion (in Brigade) reached Venizel about 1.00 a.m. Here the R.E. reconnoitering officer reported that one of the four charges laid by the Germans beneath the bridge had failed to explode and one girder remained across which it was possible to pass troops in single file. The Brigadier, therefore, made a personal examination, and decided to take the risk of transporting his troops over a section of concrete roadway from under which the girders had been blown away

The Brigade again moved forward across the bridge, breaking step and moving slowly in single file at two pace intervals. The 1st Hants led, followed by the Rifle Brigade, Somersets, and E. Lancs. It was a tedious process but covered by an advanced party of the Hants the crossing was safely accomplished, the Somersets getting across by 2.00 a.m. Ammunition carts were unloaded and the supplies were manhandled across. An hour later the whole Brigade was assembled north of the river.

In order to hold the crossing at Venizel effectively the Brigadier considered it necessary to seize the heights above Bucy-le-Long, which dominated the bridge and the flat ground between those heights and the river. General Hunter-Weston's orders were, perhaps, the briefest on record. "You see there are three bumps in front of you." He then detailed a battalion to attack each bump and kept one in reserve.

The Brigade then fixed bayonets and advanced to the attack. The Hants were ordered to take the central spur on which La Montaigne Farm was situated; the Somerset Light Infantry the left spur northwest of Bucy and the Rifle Brigade the right spur north of St. Marguerite; the 1st E. Lancs were kept in reserve.

"Thanks to the boldness of the movement," said General Hunter-Weston in his report, "it was completely successful and the heights were seized and entrenched without opposition, the enemy making no attempt to hold the trenches they had dug on the flat ground overlooking the bridge.".

(*Adapted from History*)

We started off at 10.00 a.m. feeling rested but many of us had got internal chills from the wetting we had had on the previous day. I was now in command of 'B' Company and felt glad of a horse. Prowse commanding the Battalion. We had had no rations the previous day nor did we get any today as 'A' Company had stopped the wagon to take off their rations at La Ecole and it had been held up. We had three quarters of an hour's halt in the middle of the day, but

otherwise were marching all day and it came on to pour with rain in the afternoon. Many of the men suffering from diarrhea, but they stuck to the march wonderfully. Reached Venizel about 8 p.m. after about 25 miles march. All villages we had passed through had been strewn with furniture etc. left by the Germans. We noticed an old gramophone and some records left on the road outside one village. We hoped to stop at Venizel for the night but we were turned out at 10.00 p.m. still pouring with rain and we remained halted on the road in the village till about midnight.
   (*W Whittuck*)

14th September

The Battalion was ordered to bivouac in its present position and spent a cold night on the hilltop. Guns were brought up today and the German guns were shelled. Battalion H.Q. took up their residence in a large cave. Cold and rainy.

The Battalion was now established in a sunken lane overlooking the village of Crouay, with Soissons rather to the left rear. Throughout the day the warm sun enabled the men to dry their clothes and after a good meal, prepared from sheep, bread and vegetables requisitioned locally, and a sleep, officers and men alike recovered marvelously from the fatigues through which they had recently passed.

   In spite of heavy hostile shelling throughout the day no casualties were suffered by the Somersets, indeed so far as the Battalion was concerned the Battle of the Aisne was quite a mild affair. Although the official despatches make no reference, the infantry of the 11th Brigade of the 4th Division were the first to cross the Aisne and establish positions north of the river. The positions taken up on the night of the 13th/14th were held continuously until the B.E.F. left the Aisne for the Ypres–Bethune area. (*History*)

We then had one of the worst night marches I remember, having checks and at other times racing along. The men were pretty well done and it was evident they had not much in them. We crossed the Aisne just before light by a single bridge girder. It was nervous work and took time as we could only go in single file. We reached Bucy La Long just as it was getting light and were sent on to

From:	11th Brigade
To:	Somerset Light Infantry
Time:	0905

You are being reinforced by one compnay Hants and one company East Lancs. Hold on at all costs

occupy the high ground. This did not look much like an attack at dawn and I think it was just as well the ridge tops were not occupied, as the men were dead tired. We only saw a party of Uhlans on top of the ridge as we reached the top and they disappeared at once. Prowse came up later and told me the points he particularly wanted me to guard and gave me the direction in case of further advance. I posted groups to guard these points and withdrew my Company to a bank running along the edge of a wood just below the crest of the ridge. We were shelled pretty heavily in the afternoon and I at once started the men on to digging pits with their light entrenching tools. Three of my men were killed, I had posted them to keep touch with 'C' Company on my left. We were hold-ing a wide extent of front and it did not seem probable to me that we could remain in such a position. We were all expecting a further advance. The day was bitterly cold and my feet felt like stones directly I sat down. In the evening we had orders to hold on to the position at all costs, Prowse being in command of that section of the line.

(*W Whittuck*)

Eventually by a forced march the high ground of Soissons was reached and the German shells found them. They were told to rush for some sheltered woods in the rear. 'It was awful', said Nash 'I don't know how we got through. As we ran for shelter the shells seemed to burst right in front of our faces. We only had three killed and thirty wounded, but I cannot say how the rest of us came through. I will never forget it.' When the storm of shrapnel had ceased the company set about digging trenches, which they left before they had been completed. The trenches formed a network so that they were able to walk a mile under shelter.

(*Somerset County Gazette*)

Moved off later at 2.00 p.m. to join the battalion we had not seen for five days. It was in position on top of a high ridge above the village of Bucy-le-long. From here the Germans had to be pushed out, as they were able to dominate the river and flat ground over which we had passed. The enemy was well entrenched and loath to give up this position. I took twelve men down to the village to draw rations and then got down to a nap. Later, in the middle of the night, I heard a shot and a scream. It was one of my section who had been wan-dering about and was shot at by a sentry. Fortunately the bullet only grazed his arm, but he was a startled man. Heavy showers during the night, which made things very uncomfortable.

(*Arthur Cook*)

Chapter Five

In the Trenches
15th September–4th October

15th September

Day spent in organization of defences. Shelter trenches dug by all companies. A howitzer battery which had taken up position just north of Bucy le Long church was put out of action today by German 8" howitzers.

> Some of the enemy guns, about two and a half miles from the British lines, could not be located, and were doing a lot of damage. Sergeant Archer said he did not believe that the firing came from what appeared to be a gun in the distance. Captain Jones Mortimer thought the same thing, and the matter was referred to the Colonel, with the result that the Captain and the Sergeant, under the cover of darkness, started on a perilous journey to locate the guns. This occupied them over six hours, and they found that the thing which had appeared to be a gun was a piece of pole between two wheels, and the hind leg of a horse with the hoof on it. They subsequently discovered the active guns, and knocked four or five men senseless. Returning to the trenches they were able in the morning to direct the fire which put the enemy guns out of action. (Sergeant Archer was later awarded the D.C.M.)
> (*Newspaper Cutting*)

From:	4th Division
To:	11th Brigade
Time:	1005

Instructions have been received from C-in-C that offensive action should cease temporarily unless suitable opportunities occur locally

At about 12 midday the Germans hit a house opposite the church with a high explosive shell of large calibre, completely demolishing the house. It also set on fire the East Lancs, machine-gun limber, which happened to be standing under cover of the house, and killed one horse and wounded another very badly. I happened to be near the house when it was hit, as I was told to carry up 16,000 rounds of ammunition to the trenches. The road up was blocked with debris in many places, and the church was hit. A wall had been blown down across the road in one place, and a big tree in another place. On my way up I saw a howitzer battery, which had taken up its position on the hillside in a field due west of La Montague Farm, completely put out of action by German 8.4" howitzers. The shells fell amongst the guns with surprising accuracy, in one case lifting an ammunition wagon up in the air and dropping it upside down. All the way up to the Battalion I was pursued by rifle bullets, which for some inexplicable reason came from the rear. When I returned to the church again I found out the reason. The limber, which had caught fire, was full of belts of ammunition, and the rounds were going off in regular volleys. These bullets damaged two of my S.A.A. carts, and in one case smashed a wheel.
(*G Prideaux*)

Next morning there was a pleasant surprise and that was news of food – fresh meat. We started cooking it at once but our proper rations came before we had finished and I shall never forget the delight of that tot of rum, I felt fit for anything then. Owing to shortage of N.C.O.s I could only put young ones in charge of my advanced posts. They disturbed us extremely during the day by all sorts of wild reports and retiring but, in the end, they were pacified. Things were quieter in the evening, though the shelling was pretty heavy, but we had dug better pits. When it got dark I buried the three men who had been killed soon after my arrival on the ridge, but it was sickening work with a tool no larger than a gardening trowel.
(*W Whittuck*)

At 4.00 a.m. my platoon had to go forward and occupy an advanced post We had not been there long before shrapnel was bursting over us and at 7.30 a.m. there was heavy fire in all directions. French Colonials are on our left and are a bit of a nuisance, for their movements are giving away our position and getting us strafed. They put out a machine gun section just in front of us, but shellfire drove them out of it. I saw two French officers and their horses near us. This was a foolish thing to do, for the officers got under cover, but their nags – one of them held by a man of my platoon – were in the open. Shortly afterwards a shell burst right in front of the horses. One was badly hit and had to be shot. The other took flight and could not be found. Our man had a marvellous escape, but several others were slightly wounded. The French officers looked awfully upset. We were sniped all day and there is no chance of retaliation for our field of fire only extends 200

yards ahead. The ground beyond that slopes towards the enemy and conceals his movements.
(*Arthur Cook*)

16th September

Fine day. Improved shelter trenches and fire trenches and got quite comfortable. A French battery came into action in front of 'B' Company's trenches. It was soon located by a German aeroplane and was heavily shelled. Several shells burst in 'B' Companies trenches, and casualties occurred among officers and men who happened to be outside the trenches. 2nd Lieutenant Read and 4 men were killed and Lieutenant Newton and 5 men wounded. In the morning there had been some alarm owing to a Small Arms Ammunition cart being hit and exploding cartridges in all directions. 2nd Lieutenant Read and others buried at 7.00 p.m today.

> A French Battery in rear of us sent up a section of guns which took up a position actually just in front of our trenches. They did some wonderful shooting, but as I was afraid, drew fire on to us. We were unluckily just outside our dugouts when they opened fire first. Poor Read was killed just as he made a dive for our dugout, I being just behind him. Poor Newton caught another burst just as be ran in afterwards end was very badly wounded, but I managed to get him under cover. We did not get anything quite so near afterwards, luckily, as there was no room for me. I was so sorry to lose them both, as we had got on well together and they were a great help and never too tired to go out on any reconnaissance or visiting groups. Four men were killed and eight wounded, but I managed to get stretchers up when the shells were not quite so thick. We buried Read and the four men the same night, a parson reading the service.
> (*W Whittuck*)

> We put up trip wires in front of the trenches when evening came, in case Jerry tries to give us a visit. They will help us to welcome him in a proper manner.
> (*Arthur Cook*)

17th September

Miserable day, cold and wet. Troops managed to keep fairly dry in their dugouts. Bucy le Long was heavily shelled all day by German 8.2" guns. Much damage done to buildings including 11th Brigade H.Q. Also many casualties amongst our transport horses and drivers. Brigade H.Q. was moved as a result of this shelling. There must be spies in the village. We appear to have no guns to reply to German 8".

From:	11th Brigade
To:	**Somerset Light Infantry, East Lancs, Dublin Fusiliers**
Time:	**0345**

Remember that Chivres hill is in the possession of the enemy and that he may fire at our line from south point of that hill. Dig so that you are secure from fire from this point.

About 11 a.m. the Germans started to bombard Bucy village with their 8.2" howitzers, which throw a shell of 290lb. filled with high explosive. This bombardment lasted for 1 hour 10 minutes and was the severest we had undergone. They hit both the houses on the other side of the road to mine, setting one on fire. In fact, nearly every house in the main street was hit. Many civilians were killed as well as soldiers, and a great number were wounded or, properly speaking, mutilated, as these shells were so big that if a fragment of them hit you it would cut off your head or limbs. There was a pause of about an hour in the bombardment, during which I had my dinner. About 1.30 p.m. it recommenced and went on till dusk. About 3.00 p.m. both our houses were blown up, and one of the cooks, who was inside at the time, had his foot blown off. We took shelter in a large cellar and I collected a lot of civilians, and women, and children, and sent them into the cellar. The hospital was hit three times and one wing was totally destroyed, luckily only one wounded man being killed. Two shells went into Brigade Headquarters. Nearly every house had been hit by the evening, and hundreds of horses had been killed. Luckily only two of mine had been hit, but two bolted. To show the force of explosion of these shells, one shell fell into a yard and blew to bits 7 horses and 6 men, smashed in the back wall of the house in front and blew two men, who were in the house, into the street. They were not hurt, only shaken, but they were quite black from the smoke.
(*G Prideaux*)

When I was first wounded, my leg was badly shot up, I was carried into a hospital but I had not been there many minutes when the Germans began to shell the hospital although the Red Cross flag was waving over it. For protection we had to be carried into the cellars where we stayed about five hours. Then we were put into an automobile, which took us to a train in which we remained for four days and four nights. Then the American ambulance came and I was not sorry when I got to this place – The American Military Hospital, Neuilly sur Seine.
(*Private T Wevell, Bath Chronicle*) *Private Wevell subsequently died from his wounds.*

18th September

Fine day 'B' Company shelled again today, several casualties. Major Prowse appointed O.C. left subsection with the Battalion and 2 companies East Lancs under him. Rifle Brigade in reserve. Very bad night, rained in torrents.

From:	11th Brigade
To:	**Rifle Brigade, Hampshires, East Lancs, Somerset L.I**
Time:	**0707**

Hostile aeroplanes may be fired at provided that the order to do so is given by an officer who should satisfy himself before giving the order that the plane is hostile.

Having an opportunity to wash my feet I tried to take my socks off, but had to call for assistance. It took four men to get them off! Having to keep our boots on all through the retreat has not improved our feet. After washing my socks I had to put the blighters on again as I had no others. They had shrunk to half their normal size, but after an effort I got them back again. 'B' Company had nine men wounded by shellfire today.
(*Arthur Cook*)

I shouldn't at all mind being home for a few days, it must lovely to be certain of your next meal at a fixed time, and decent clothes and a dry bed, but on the whole I am really enjoying it very much. I suppose I have slept in wet clothes pretty nearly as often as in dry ones; at first wet with sweat, and the last few days from rain, but I am as fit as is possible for anyone to be.
(*Edward Packe*)

19th September

Cold northwest wind, fine. No change in the situation in our immediate vicinity. G.O.C. decided to place field gun in our line to flank ground in front of 'D' Company's trenches. This was brought up tonight and dug in during the night.

Filthy wet. Had get an 18lb field gun put up near my post, did not finish until 12.30 a.m. Too wet to turn in so walked about soaked. Went and dug into a cave where it was dry.
(*F S Bradshaw*)

The Zouaves (French North African troops) based about 100 yards from the Somersets crawled some 400 yards through sugar beet taking three or four hours to cover the distance. But being rewarded by complete surprise to the Germans everyone of whom they killed without firing a shot. The Zouaves displayed a particular liking for British bully beef and were always ready to make exchanges for it.

(*R Nash, Somerset County Gazette*)

Devonport. An inquest was held on Private Walter Joyce, 1st Somerset Light Infantry. Private Joyce accompanied his Battalion to the front and was invalided home with a bad foot.

Private Frank Upham said on Saturday evening as he was going to his room about 8.30 p.m. he heard a shot. He ran into the room and found Joyce on the floor dead, a rifle by his side. Private Fred Oakham said he met Joyce at Taunton Railway station on Saturday. He seemed worried about his foot and asked if he thought he would get into trouble for being sent home. Witness told him he would not, as he was being invalided home. Dr R.J. Thomas, medical officer in charge of Bull Point Barracks said Joyce's foot had probably been bad through a poisoned ingrowing toenail. Between Joyce's knees was a blood stained envelope on which the deceased had written in pencil. "As I am unable to march I will be no good as a soldier. England will win."

The jury returned a verdict of "Suicide whilst of unsound mind" and expressed deep sympathy with the widow and relatives.

(*Pulmans Weekly*)

20th September

No change in situation. 3rd Reinforcement under Lieutenant Vincent (93 N.C.O.s and men) arrived tonight.

Poured with rain in the morning as usual. Went to church on the hill. Cleared up in the afternoon. One of 'B' Company shot himself in foot. Went forward to Company position and saw German positions. About 7.30 p.m. very heavy rifle fire was heard all along our position which lasted about twenty minutes. A Corporal of French artillery reported three French spies caught in the village. The village is full of them which, no doubt, accounts for the German excellent artillery practice. Neate and I got up our valises by supply train. Got a wash and clean clothing. What a relief, had not changed or taken off our clothes since 5th.

(*G Prideaux*)

I will try and give you a typical day at present. We have 'outlook' by day, every other day and night. Sentry every other night, runs to about an hour a man. Night sentry work is very exciting as you can see nothing and have to trust entirely to your ears. We 'stand to arms' at 4.40 a.m. (i.e. wake up and get your stuff handy in case of a sudden attack.). At 5.30 a.m. we light fires and a party goes down for the day's rations consisting of a little bacon, plenty of Bully Beef, sometimes bread, but if not biscuit, 1lb pot of jam between six men, cheese, and tea and sugar. We then cook our bacon and have breakfast. After

this there is a fatigue party to fetch water from the village and this generally gives one the opportunity to loot some spuds. At about 11.00 a.m the mail is generally given out (for last week at any rate). Lunch is the item of importance. The mail goes out a 1.30 p.m, then tea comes at 4.30 p.m and we generally retire to our holes at about 7.00 p.m. So you see we are pretty well making up for the rough time we had to start with.
(*Edward Packe*)

Nash confirms the fact that British troops fared well as far as food was concerned. Every morning for up to three weeks and two days the section had bacon for breakfast. There was sometimes a hazardous journey to fetch it as the enemy swept the area between the trenches and the village on the rear slope in which the British quartermaster's stores were situated. But the day's rations having been obtained the half company not on duty in the advanced trench for 24 hours, fried the bacon beside the woods which sheltered the sleeping trench. They complained that the enemy had not wished them a good morning unless the meal was accompanied by a bit of shrapnel. The bacon for breakfast was followed by stew for dinner and jam for tea, so that if they were wet through for days there was certainly no shortage of food.
(*Somerset County Gazette*)

21st–23rd September

No change in situation. French brigade on our left made two demonstrations against Perriere Farm without success, during this period. We stood to arms but had no orders to advance ourselves, only to resist counter-attack if one was launched.

21st. Relieved No. 4 platoon in the forward copse. Some one – I believe Sergeant Wilcox – went up one of the trees for observation and reported Germans walking towards us. We could hear the Germans talking quite plainly but could not see them. They moved away to our right much to our relief. The boys had an ounce of tobacco and a box of matches per section. Matches are very scarce and difficult to obtain. There is a German gun that comes very close to our front, fires about six shots and hops it again. I think it must be a motor lorry.
(*Arthur Cook*)

23rd. About 11 o'clock, suddenly tremendous artillery and rifle fire broke out in the French lines, and was promptly answered by the Germans. It was a clear bright night. Both combatants were sending up rockets. Searchlights were throwing their sinister glare on the opposite hill sides. Soissons, in the valley below, was being shelled. This lasted about an hour, when everything became still and quiet.

On sentry from midnight to 2.00 a.m. French supposed to be making an attack at dawn but nothing happens. 'A' Company of ours nearly fired on by

mistake. Ordered to fix bayonets when we go out to the copse in the evening, also to carry two pieces of corrugated iron roofing per man, making a hell of a noise but nothing happens.
(*Edward Packe*)

24th–26th September

4th Reinforcement under 2nd Lieutenants Glossop and Turner arrived. No change in situation.

From:	4th Division
To:	11th Brigade
Time:	1148

Following received from III Corps reads:
In view of the constant mistakes which are being made in firing on British aeroplanes the G.O.C. desires that the task of engaging hostile aeroplanes on the right bank of the River Aisne shall for the present be left to the anti aircraft guns which are now in position.

There are some Algerian troops on out left and they are awfully amusing. They shoot at any blooming thing that moves. One day they got tired of sitting in their trenches so they arranged an attack on their own, without saying a word to their officers, so at dawn they sallied out and of course suffered enormous losses but, I believe, gave the Germans something to chew. One of them came back to our lines with a bayonet wound in his leg and one of our officers noted his haversack was bulging very much and also very 'jammy'; so he asked what he had got in there. The Algerian said 'Souvenir, Souvenir' and displayed in his haversack a German helmet and head! Although I didn't actually see this, I only saw the chap come in and I believe it's absolutely true.
(*Edward Packe*)

The artillery fire, Nash says, was at times terrific, the only difference between Sundays and other days was that it seemed heavier on the former. One Sunday a church parade had been arranged but had to be abandoned on account of the severity of the cannonade. On another Sunday there was a voluntary service and in a natural hollow some seventy of the Somersets attended, well known hymns being sung to a strange and fearsome accompaniment.
(*Somerset County Gazette*)

The Zouaves are just overlapping us and are on the edge of the same plateau and were always trying to attack across the open and lost very heavily. The French General kept telling me that we must get on too, so finally, I took my

From:	11th Brigade
To:	Left sub-section, Somerset Light Infantry
Time:	1926

A deep cut trench is required on the northwest side of the knoll in front of your haystack observation post, 1/2 mile east of y in Croy.

This observation post to contain about three men to be deep cut so as to be proof against shellfire. The position to be reached from the ground on our side of the ridge by a communicating trench running generally at right angles to our line.

From:	11th Brigade
To:	4th Division
Time:	1538
	Confidential

I have been to see the G.O.C. 90th French Brigade. His companies on our left have made trenches about 100 to 150 yards in front of their former position. Their right is only about 100 yards west of Captain Jones Mortimor's post at head of ravine; the intervening ground is swept by fire from Captain Watson's post on our spur. I am arranging to cover this 100 yards by close support from the ravine at night. The GOC 90th Brigade is satisfied with these dispositions.

He confidentially informs me that as long as the Germans hold their dominating positions west and northeast it is impossible for the French to maintain themselves at Le Perriere farm even if he can take it. He has already captured it but has been driven out with great loss of life by machine gun and artillery fire. He thinks it folly to advance over the open plain just where the enemy are strongest and, confidentially is sarcastic over the French higher staff who never come to see the situation themselves

General over to see him. We had two bottles of Champagne and a melon and both Generals agreed it was madness to attack. The French said he wished the Divisional Generals in the rear would come and look at the ground and not just say "Allez! Avancez!" so they aren't going to try again.
(*G R Parr, acting as Brigade Liaison Officer*)

26th. We had orders to dig an advanced post by night in front of our haystack and about 500 yards in front of our original trench. This post was therefore to be absolutely exposed and manned day and night. We worked with a covering party, but being in a root field and very damp, we did not get on very quickly with the work. We worked on it three nights and completed about 300 yards of communication trench when it was manned by a section. The first night soon alter dark, the section ran away, saying that there were thousands of Germans advancing and whole regiments of cavalry. There certainly had been a burst or two of rifle fire. I was sent out with twenty men to clear up the

Figure 4a
Officer's Dugout, Aisne. (*Contemporary Magazine*)

Figure 4b
Trenches, Aisne. (*Contemporary Magazine*)

situation. It sounded very nice, but I did not quite know what I was going to do if the enemy were in force. It was a bright moonlight night and as soon as we got on top of the ridge we were fired on from about 80 yards away. Of course, we showed up clearly against the moon. I had arranged beforehand that all my men were to drop when they saw me lie down. I crawled forward with the scouts to see if I could find out anything, but all was quiet. I then went back and found that my men had retired, two being wounded as the

result of moving. I managed to bring them up again, and we were again fired on, but we managed to get over the ridge with a rush and lie down without damage. I went forward again with three men and reconnoitered to within 100 yards of enemy's trenches, but everything was quiet and I reported that there can only have been an enemy patrol about. I certainly did not see the thousands of Germans advancing though I remained out for about four hours.
(*W Whittuck*)

27th September

French made a slight advance during night on spur north of Erquy, and were heavily shelled by Germans at dawn. They clung on however. Captain Yatman 'D' Company ordered to make forward observation post northwest of haystack. This was done during the night and a communication trench dug out to it.

Rather a lot of shelling this morning. Fed up with this place and want to get on. Had to rebuke my subaltern twice for being too noisy.
(*F S Bradshaw*)

I was very much amused to see in last week's Times account of how 'a heavy pall of black smoke hung over the cannons'. As a matter of fact there is very little smoke at all and what there is clears away very soon, and then it is white smoke. Shrapnel bursting makes a white smoke, Lyddite a yellow smoke and cordite a dirty brown. The German and English shells passing over our heads so we know something about it. One day the Germans were firing a big gun

From:	Somerset Light Infantry, Major Prowse
To:	11th Brigade
Date:	27th September 1914

Captain Yatman returned from digging the new observation post northwest of Haystack at dawn this morning. He reports that a very long communicating trench was necessary and that this has not yet been completed. Whilst the work was in progress he reconnoitered the front and found a sunken fence under cover of which the enemy can approach to within 20 yards of the new post without being seen. He further reports movement at Mauberge road near enemy's haystack early this morning apparently from east to west. I have been to our haystack this morning and have also previously made a personal reconnaissance from 'A' company post. I observed that from the latter a gully runs up in front of new observation post that is probably the sunken fence referred to by Captain Yatman. This I intend to verify if possible by a patrol this evening. By day 'A' post in pit can fire up their gully for some 600 yards.

battery (I believe about 108lb shell) and they came over six at a time nearly all day. We (the infantry) were as safe as houses because they were trying for our artillery and the shells were all bursting about a quarter of a mile behind us. (*Edward Packe*)

28th September

Brigadier came up this morning to arrange some form of advance to keep up with French on our left. He decided entrenching a line which was more in line with the French, fatigue parties commenced the new trenches.

A little sniping during the night, nothing else exciting. Not quite so cold, but cloudy, looks like rain. Hunter-Weston worrying us to go further out, which we think is unnecessary. Went out at 6.00 p.m. to dig trenches further out, was sniped at but no one hit. Came in at 1.00 a.m. (*F S Bradshaw*)

29th September

Quiet day, very little shelling. Machine gun section hit a German aeroplane, but didn't do much damage. Preparations for a German attack were reported and the section stood to arms. An officer's patrol could not confirm this report and no attack was made on us.

My trenches are a dream, as made by my men. Officers of other brigades and officers also of the French Army, who are in touch with us, on my left, come round to see them as one of the sights. They are dry, roomy, comfortable,

From:	Somerset Light Infantry
To:	11th Brigade
Time:	1157

Have been visited by Colonel Ancel commanding 3rd Regiment Zouaves de Marche whose Headquarters are at Crouy. He has relieved the Tunisian Tirailleurs during the night and his dispositions are one battalion lining the ridge from Pit Post to Mauberge Road along crest and one battalion on slope west of railway southeast slope of Pt 132. One battalion in reserve at Crouy.

    I pointed out to him our dispositions and how our wire defences run.

    Apparently he wishes to attack the Perriere Farm position single-handed.

His regiment belongs to 89th Brigade commanded by General Trafford whose Headquarters are at St Paul.

    C B Prowse

roofed and in fact almost cosy. The men give their different posts and trenches definite names such as "Woodbine Villa", "Wheatsheaf Inn", or such and such a trench. They are very proud of their work and very happy. The sick rate in these trenches north of Bucy was less than in our barracks at Colchester. I look after my men though I work them hard.
(*Brigadier General Hunter-Weston*)

30th September

Cool overcast day. No change in our situation. French 3rd Zouaves commenced attack on Perriere Farm at 3.00 p.m. Made very little progress. One British howitzer battery and French field battery formed only artillery support.

A man of 'D' Company was shot dead by a sentry last night. Artillery active today. We can see some of our shells as they scream over us. They look like a large cricket ball in the air and you can follow their flight for a long way. Disturbed this morning by a rumbling noise and moaning. A trench shelter had fallen in on top of four men. A Lance Corporal was badly hurt and sent to hospital.
(*Arthur Cook*)

From:	11th Brigade
To:	**Rifle Brigade, Hampshires, East Lancs, Somerset L.I**
Time:	**1015**

Brigadier General is desirous that all officers of the battalions should profit from the experience of entrenching under active service conditions, which is now afforded by our section of defence. He is of the opinion that most of the work is now executed is admirable. He directs therefore that commanding officers will go round the whole section of defence with half the officers of their battalion today and with the other half tomorrow pointing out for instruction purposes good and bad points of various works.

From:	11th Brigade
To:	**Rifle Brigade, Hampshires, East Lancs, Somerset L.I**
Time:	**1020**

In view of an advance and in order to ensure the men being physically fit for marching, the Brigadier General directs that all officers, N.C.O.s and men who are not employed in trench work should be exercised by route marching through the village and in climbing up and down the ravines at the back of our position.

From:	**Brigadier General Hunter Watson**
To:	**Major Prowse**
Time:	**1547**

Try and find out unofficially whether the French on your left really mean to press the attack home on Perriere Farm. If they seize Perriere Farm decision as to our action will probably require my presence on the hill. I do not want to come up the hill if the French attack is merely a demonstration resulting in their return to their present positions, as has been the case on previous occasions.

From:	**Somerset Light Infantry**
To:	**11th Brigade**
Time:	**1930**

Following received from Commandant 3rd Zouaves.

Very slight progress on the plateau in direction of Perriere farm. I have pushed forward four companies who have stopped on the edge of the wood at 100 metres from level crossing which is in front of the Mill of Sous La Perriere. It would be necessary to concentrate fire on this point D'Appli (two houses which are at the level crossing and the mill which is 70 metres behind). These two points are strongly held.

One solitary death from a stray bullet during our more or less quiet life here (on the Aisne) casts a gloom over us all. Private Sliny, C–'s servant, was hit while carrying tea from the cooking place to the officers. He was buried with military honours next day; his platoon paid their last tribute to this gallant man.
(*W Watson*)

1st October

Fine and hot day. In afternoon parties of officers inspected the trenches prepared by other battalions. A fine view of the enemy's trenches was obtained from those near La Montagne Farm prepared by the Dublin Fusiliers and, also from an observation post dug by Capt. Yatman's Company. Orders were issued in the evening for a change in the dispositions of the troops.

Build up trenches that had fallen in. Maxims fire at German aeroplane and I guide the belts in for both of them, the guns being cocked up at a high angle, the only result of our firing was to render me quite deaf.
(*Edward Packe*)

2nd October

Cold day. Foggy early morning. Scotch mist most of the day

'H' Company were successful last night in accounting for six Germans under the following circumstances. At about 10.00 p.m Corporal Windsor in charge of 'H' Company's observation post saw a party of about 20 Germans approaching from the northeast. He also saw others behind them and one is reported to have fallen into the communication trench. He waited till they were within 10 yards and then fired with the result stated. Others were wounded but were got away by their comrades. About one hour later a party of about 50 returned and opened fire on the trench from a distance of about 50 yards. Corporal Windsor's post replied. The result was not known. There were no losses on our side. This observation post is about 550 yards in front of our main trenches and about 1000 yards from the German trenches. An excellent view of their position is obtained from it, but it is rather liable to be cut off at night. During the following night (Oct2nd/3rd), R.E constructed wire entanglements west of the post and 'H' Company placed wire ladders etc. around the post to lessen the risk of it's being surrounded.

> It was the turn of my platoon to occupy the advanced post, and having a good reliable sergeant, Windsor, I sent him out and stopped out for some time myself. I had just got back and had something to eat when there was certainly quite a heavy fire. I got out as soon as possible with another section and found my section absolutely elated having as they said killed about 20 Germans. It

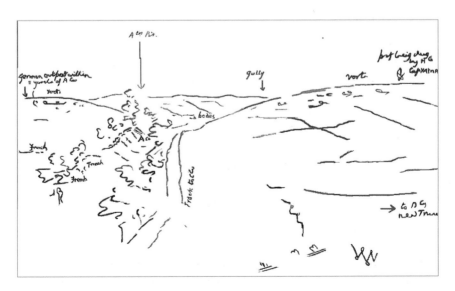

Figure 5
Sketch of the Somersets Positions, Aisne. (WO95 1496)

was a strong German patrol that had surrounded the post and tried to get at them from in rear by the communication trench. I was very pleased, as it had proved to the men that there was no necessity to run away and being in a trench they were much better off than any Germans advancing in the open. I was particularly amused at one man who was too short to look over the top of the communication trench and had taken off his water bottle and pack and so had been able to see over the top and, as he told me, killed a German. Everything was quiet for the rest of the night, but before light I went out with two men and picked up five Germans.

We were now pretty well up to strength again but had about eight junior officers in place of senior officers that were badly needed. We had had a few Courts Martial and our cave was always selected for them, being so well furnished, we had even made a washstand.
(*W Whittuck*)

Field General Court Martial at Bucy le Long. Two men charged with cowardice. One found guilty and sentenced to 3 years Penal Servitude, the other being found 'Not Guilty'.
(*PRO*)

Our men also did well in beating off an attack on a post held by one Corporal Windsor and a party of 'H' Company.. They let the Germans come up and one under officer spoke to Windsor and said 'Don't shoot, I'm English'. Result five killed and others wounded judging by the howls. They brought up reinforcements and were again beaten off. The Germans were the 2nd Pomeranian Grenadiers, a crack corps. The post was christened Windsor Castle.
(*Un-named Officer, Somerset County Gazette*)

3rd October

Nothing happened during the day. At night the Royal Engineers erected a line of obstacles between the Bottomless Pit and Windsor Castle. A telephone wire was also laid between these two posts.

From:	**4th Division**
To:	**11th Brigade**
Time:	**2145**

The G.O.C. congratulates the Brigadier on the day's bag. If the last eight are not buried can you find if any of them have the Landwher cross on their headgear. If not buried tomorrow an officer is coming over early to help investigate.

During all this period we frequently had messages to say that the French were going to attack at such and such a time and that we were to support them with fire, but the attacks never came off. The Turcos did their best to keep us awake at night, as hardly a night passed without our being aroused by a tremendous fusillade and in the morning we would find that they had gained about 80 yards of ground and during the day they would retire about 200 yards, not very satisfactory for us but they were quiet about it. The Germans always fired field guns during an attack of this sort and that added to the din, but did not do much damage. A wounded Turco was brought into our dressing station one day and we noticed that he smelt very strongly. He had a German head in his haversack, which he hoped to take home to his wife. Parcels and letters were arriving regularly now and we had formed quite a well equipped little store in our cave and had made chairs and a table out of old ration boxes etc.
(*W Whittuck*)

Went out at 2.00 a.m. with two sections, covering party of Engineers doing wire entanglements. Got in about 4.30 a.m. Nothing much during the day. At 6.30 p. m. went out to the pit. Started to lay telephone to Hunter Folly but got shot at, went back and started around another way completed the line at 7.30 p.m.
(*F S Bradshaw*)

4th October

Quiet day. Nothing of importance happened.

Chapter Six

Move into Flanders
5th–18th October

5th October

2nd Lieutenants Braithwaite and Dennys joined the battalion on first appointment. About 12 noon an order was received to be prepared to move this evening. Got tools and SAA wagons packed up. 'A' and 'B' Companies (reserve Companies) ordered to move at 6.45 p.m. Headquarters and 'C' and 'D' when trenches had been handed over to the French. The French troops did not however arrive and late in the evening the order was cancelled. Cold night. Frost.

From:	11th Brigade
To:	Rifle Brigade, Hampshires, Somerset L.I
Time:	1146

Be prepared to move tonight. No supplies will arrive. Ration of the day to be issued. Every man to have iron ration. This is most important. Surplus ammunition in trenches will be brought down and stacked under instructions of Brigade Transport Officer in field west of Venizel-Bucy road just north of Bucy. 120 rounds only per man will be carried.

From:	11th Brigade
To:	Rifle Brigade, Hampshires, East Lancs, Somerset L.I
Time:	1740

Conditional instructions as to move are cancelled. East Lancs only will be prepared to move from Bucy at 1900. Other battalions will not cross the river tonight and will only retain with them machine gun wagons, cooks wagons, two SAA carts per battalion and water and tool carts. All other transport will be ready to leave at 1830, destination to be notified later. Spare ammunition now in trenches will be sent back in wagons, which will be provided. No supplies will be sent across the river tonight, except oats and the day's reserve in hand will be used

6th October

French officers came up this morning to take over trenches. 'A' and 'B' Companies left for Buzancy at 7.00 p.m. French relieving troops arrived at 10.45 p.m

> Most of first line transport moved to Septmonts. Several horses sick with strangles. Managed to make up four pairs of artillery harness. Just reached Buzancy heard a great crash and saw a column of flame. I thought it was a shell burst. Found village in a turmoil, everybody thinking it was a shell. I found that it was a guard who had struck a match on a petrol barrel which exploded nearly killing him and blowing one end of it about 50 feet up the street.
> (*G Prideaux*)

> The 'Sets' were not sorry to leave their 'mud huts' as it was getting somewhat monotonous in the trenches. The only thing fresh each day was that an outlying post of the 'Sets' might add to the heap of Germans killed just in front. The majority evidently came out to see who had been killed and the British nearly always polished them off. Directly the Somersets left the trenches the French entered them.
> (*Corporals Bailey and Barrett, Chard and Ilminster News*)

7th October

The French completed taking over by 1.00 a.m Battalion Headquarters and 'C' and 'D' Companies left Bucy Le Long at 1.30 a.m. Marched via Venizel and Septmonts to a large cave at Buzancy which held the whole battalion. A very cold night, but just managed to keep warm walking. Thursday passed fine and sunny and the battalion moved into a wood near the cave which was a more sanitary bivouac.

> After a dreary wait for the 'Sets' they marched to a large chateau about eight miles away. The place had rock caves large enough to billet the Battalion, but after they had lighted a few fires for warmth they could scarcely breathe and accordingly they moved out under some trees, this position taken up to escape the notice of aeroplanes.
> (*Corporals Bailey and Barrett, Chard and Ilminster News*)

From:	**11th Brigade**
To:	**Rifle Brigade, Hampshires, Somerset L.I**
Time:	**1031**

O.C. Battalions are reminded of the extreme importance of concealment from aircraft observation. As little movement as possible to take place.

It will also be arranged in battalions that the men remain lying down for a period of four hours so as to obtain rest and sleep during the day.

8th October

Moved at 12 midnight to billets at Plessier le Heulier. Arrived about 3.00 a.m. Extremely cold night with east wind blowing. Got about three hours sleep. No idea where going to, though imagine it must be somewhere up north east of France. Expected to stay here the night but at 12.30 p.m got orders to move at 4.00 p.m and march 17 miles. Marched at 4.35 p.m. via Crucy-Fleury-Villeurs Cotteret to Largny. Two hours halt at Fleury at 8.00 p.m. Beautiful march through forest country. Not so cold tonight. Arrived Largny 2.00 a.m. Took about an hour to get settled down in billets. Billets consisted as usual of large farm, but in this case it was not quite big enough and careful fitting in was necessary.

Roused at 7.00 a.m. parade at 10.00 a.m. for a Court Martial also have one hours musketry parade.
(*Edward Packe*)

Billeted in a farmyard finding straw as good as a feather bed to tired men. Awoke to the sound of propellers and looking up saw about 20 French aeroplanes off to reconnoitre the enemy positions. They were well behind the firing line at this time and the writers think that this must have been an aeroplane depot.
(*Corporals Bailey and Barrett, Chard and Ilminster News*)

9th October

Quite expected to stop here some time but got orders to move at 2.00 p.m. Marched to Bethisy arriving 7.00 p.m. Very comfortable but scattered billets. Headquarters very comfortable in Notary's house. Everyone very kind to troops. 2nd Lieutenant Parr went sick today with a bowel complaint.

I had the luxury of sleeping in a comfortable bed with sheets and taking all my clothes off for the second time since we had been out. The men were all very comfortable, but unfortunately some of them had too much to drink. One man I remember in particular who had volunteered for any rough job in the trenches was absolutely bowled over with drink.
(*W Whittuck*)

We slept in a brush factory surrounded by brushes.
(*A Cook*)

A treat, being allowed to go shopping for three hours and then off again.
(*Corporals Bailey and Barrett, Chard and Ilminster News*)

10th October

Heard today that we are to entrain at Compiegne. Marched from Bethisy at 1.40 p.m. Billeted at Vannette at 6.30 p.m. Mayor very good in rendering assistance to billeting party – mine quite comfortable. Got orders to start entrainment at 2.30 a.m.

> The next day we reached Compiegne, but the marches had gradually been getting longer and some of the men had very bad feet owing to worn-out and burnt boots. We had no ambulance with us, so they had to get along the best way they could and I must say most of them stuck it with one or two lifts on the transport wagons.
> (*W Whittuck*)

> The next billeting place was a ballroom in which the decorations were still hanging reminding the men of Christmas time.
> (*Corporals Bailey and Barrett, Chard and Ilminster News*)

11th October

Vehicles and horses commenced entraining at 2.30 a.m. by a party of 100 men under senior subaltern. Men arrived at the station at 4.00 a.m. Entrainment completed by 5.15 a.m. Delayed by having to remove seating accommodation prepared for men from the horseboxes. Left Compeigne 6.00 a.m., destination given as Etaples. Arrived there via Creuil and Amiens at 2.45 p.m. Ordered to go to St Omer. And arrived about 8.30 p.m. Accommodation limited as other units of the 4th Division and III Corps had to be cleared from the station, a lengthy process, so did not start detraining until 11.30 p.m.

> Arrived at Amiens, where an excellent breakfast was waiting, but just as we had started, the train began to move on, so we had to fly, damned shame.
> (*F S Bradshaw*)

> We stopped at Etaples and were given bread, tobacco, chocolate and postcards by civilians, mostly charming young ladies. They were all after souvenirs!
> (*A Cook*)

> At 2.00 a.m, boarded a train and skirted the sea for some distance. Many men's eyes turned towards England and there was a little shouting, but much thinking was done.
> (*Corporals Bailey and Barrett, Chard and Ilminster News*)

12th October

Finished at about 1.30 a.m. Delay caused by having to arrange three days supplies which had been brought up by train on two wagons. Had eventually to send back two wagons from billets for the balance. Billeted at Blendeques at 3.15 a.m. Parade at 1.00 p.m to move off in motor lorries. Very warm afternoon. The lorries (French) did not arrive until 1.00 a.m.

> Arrived at Blendeques at 3.30 a.m. and billeted. Were warned to be ready to be moved by motor lorry at 1.00 p.m. Waited on the road in the village until 11.50 p.m. Slept for a few hours at a nice house, people called Caudin. Had a good meal at the pub. Extraordinary pretty girl waited on us; she was engaged to the publican's brother. Saw a nice old brass bottle there, which I said I would fetch when the war was over, put my card on it. Left by motor lorry at 3.15 a.m.
> (*F S Bradshaw*)

> Marched half a mile to Blendeques and waited 14 hours for French motor transport to take us to Hondeghem. It was cold and wretched waiting about, so we lit a large fire, had a sing-song and told some good old yarns which cheered us up a bit.
> (*A Cook*)

> The journey concluded at night and the men waited all the next day for some motorcars to convey them to the Front. They did not arrive until about midnight and while waiting for them the party slept on the road. The motorcars in which the writers were placed broke down after travelling a considerable distance and the men in it were distributed amongst other vehicles, some riding on the mudguards. They were well wrapped up but travelling at such a pace that their fingers became numbed and they found it hard to hold on.
> (*Corporals Bailey and Barrett, Chard and Ilminster News*)

13th October

The whole Battalion was conveyed by the lorries to Hondeghem (about 13 miles). A very cold but fine night. The French drivers who took us had been doing the same job on the previous five days and nights without sleep. Breakfast, then marched at 10.00 a.m (cold rain started). Slow march with many long halts via Caestre and Fletres. 10th and 12th Brigades attacked a position not very strongly held mainly north and south through Meteren. Attack started about 1.00 p.m and continued until about 5.30 p.m. when the position was carried at the point of the bayonet. The weather was awful all afternoon, a cold rain falling in torrents. The 11th Brigade was in a turnip field west of Fletre where all got wet through. About 6.00 p.m the Battalion was ordered to occupy a position about 1200 yards in the rear of the captured Meteren position to cover the guns. The position was reconnoitered and occupied by about 8.00 p.m. 'C' and 'H' Companies furnished outposts. 'A' and 'B' in reserve in farm. Expected to get no food and were agreeably surprised to get a splendid supper provided in a farm. Whole battalion dug themselves in during night.

We had a very cold ride and. after a lot of muddle and buses breaking down arrived near Hasbrouck where we found that our own transport and cooks had been doing outposts for us during the night. After a hasty breakfast we moved on in the direction of Fletre. It came on to pour with rain and it was miserable work waiting about whilst there was sharp fighting going on in our front. As it grew dark Company Commanders moved forward to select a position for outposts. I had to leave my horse which was stolen by a Bombardier, but I got it back next day with a greatcoat and blanket into the bargain.
(*W Whittuck*)

The lorries arrived at 2.30 a.m. We embussed near the Church and reached Hondeghem at 6.30 a.m. It was a very rough journey and we were glad to get out and stretch our limbs. We had breakfast in a field. While there a man accidentally shot himself in the foot! Marched at 10.00 a.m. through Caestre to a village beyond and formed up in mass formation on a ploughed field. We rested on the ground while it rained in torrents. We laid down flat and covered ourselves with ground sheets.
(*A Cook*)

14th October

Trenches improved this morning. Bailleul, reported on the previous day as being held by strong forces of the enemy was found to be evacuated and, at 10.00 a.m. the town was entered by the III Corps. The Battalion was ordered to move at 11.00 a.m and marched through Meteren to Bailleul. Very cold but not much rain. Got into billets in Lunatic Asylum at about 9.00 p.m. after a slow march of about four miles.

Moved up through village ahead of Main Body. Waited for a long time on the road, advanced twice a few hundred yards then got into village of Bailleul and waited there until about 7.30 a.m. Then by degrees we managed to get into quite a good billet at the Asylum Farm along with the Hampshires, it was rather crowded. Had to put a picket out at fork roads, was told by Regimental Staff it was only a few hundred yards down, they generally say that, of course it was over a mile out.
(*F S Bradshaw*)

I was given a new shirt, the first I have had in France. Moved off at 1.00 p.m. through Meteren. There must have been a great street fight here. Many dead horses and cows lying about. The enemy seems to be in hurried retreat. Halted in Bailleul for two hours. The people very kind and gave us plenty to eat and drink. Their joy at seeing us on the heels of the hated invader was unbounded.

Billeted for the night in some very fine stables at Bailleul.
(*A Cook*)

15th October

Had good nights rest. Remained in billets until noon when moved out to 1 mile east of Bailleul in support of East Lancs. Were told we should probably return to billets for the night and were ordered to do so at 4.30 p.m. On way back, however a message was received to march to Cros Ros north of Rabot on the Nieppe road. Arrived about 6.30 p.m. Orders as follows were issued by the G.O.C. 11th Brigade. Hants supported by East Lancs to attack and capture Nieppe, Somerset L.I supported by Rifle Brigade to endeavour to get across the bridge over River Lys at Erquinghem; or failing that to dig in north of the bridge. This column was under the command of Major Prowse. The column marched at about 11.00 p.m in the following order. Somerset Light Infantry, Rifle Brigade M.G. sections 4 S.A.A. carts, 4 tool carts, 7 Company R.E. No opposition was encountered when the head reached Les Trois Tilleurs, so a halt was made and a patrol under Lieutenant Bush went forward to the bridge at Erquinghem to reconnoiter.

Some Bavarians captured in the town yesterday; say that they are very fed up with the war. I suppose our job now is to clear the Germans out of Belgium. They seem to have made a very hasty retreat from St Omer.
(*F S Bradshaw*)

Had a look round at some of the German trenches and found they were only sham ones with mangels stuck on top at intervals to look like heads. We had a bit of a smile at this! At noon we were ordered to do covering party to the

From:	**Brigadier General Hunter Weston**
To:	**Somerset Light Infantry**
Time:	**2310**

Orders have arrived from III Corps that the river is not to be crossed tonight. You will hold strongly the railway at 3/4 mile southwest of Nieppe and the road junction 1/4 m southwest of Halte with posts thrown out in front of these. The road junction at La Menegate will also be held by you. This latter post the 6th Division will probably take over from you later. Send a patrol forward with an engineer officer accompanying to Erquinghem bridge to see if it is held and report on condition, the engineer officer should if possible get an idea of the material required to put it in a state of repair. He should report also on the condition of the roads and their fitness for wheeled traffic.

    Reconnoitre alternative position for getting infantry across the river than the bridge and also for pontoon or trestle bridge.

Hampshires while reconnoitring the enemy. Returned to billets at 4.30 p.m. when we were suddenly ordered to advance.

We went forward four or five miles, the latter part with fixed bayonets. The dogs were a nuisance. Every house we passed seemed to have a dog which barked, warning the enemy what was afoot. Two large fires in front showed up for miles. An outpost was left and we went back two and a half miles to a farm. (*A Cook*)

16th October

At about 2.30 a.m the patrol returned and reported the bridge intact but cleverly prepared for defence. They had however not crossed and did not know whether the bridge was held. At this hour an officer of the 11th Brigade Staff came out to say that orders had been received that the river was not to be crossed that night. This relieved Major Prowse of the onus of deciding whether to try to cross or not. After events showed that the crossing would probably have been attended with great loss of life as it was covered from well-concealed trenches and obstacles were numerous. Another patrol under 2nd Lieutenant Glossop crossed the bridge about 5.00 a.m and found the enemy had just retired from the bridgehead trenches. The two battalions accordingly went into billets at about 3.00 a.m, the Rifle Brigade returning to La Creche. The Somerset Light Infantry being disposed with outposts on the line Halte-La Menegate. Two companies in support about the level crossing 600 yards northwest of the Halte. The remainder of the day was quiet. In the evening the line was pushed forward to the line L'Hallobeau-Les Trois Tilleurs. A quiet night.

> Occupied the bridge at Erquinghem, went to end of village and Glossop's party killed two. Crowds of Belgian refugees trying to get back.
> (*F S Bradshaw*)

From:	11th Brigade
To:	4th Division
Time:	1221

The advance party of Somerset Light Infantry has crossed Erquinghem Bridge and are holding the junction of the roads just south of the bridge. As the patrol crawled up to the bridge from the west three German cavalry who were holding the trench got on their horses and rode off to the east.

The patrol pushing on found the bridge, which had been barricaded and entangled and strongly entrenched to the west, unoccupied. The inhabitants say that the garrison of this bridge, which had been held strongly with machine gun and cannon, cleared off finally this morning, asking the way to Lille. The inhabitants declare that Armentieres is practically clear of the enemy

All mounted officers ride over and cross frontier into Belgium and drink to our success at wayside inn. Sir John French motors past.
(*W Watson*)

The next night the 'Sets' advanced very quietly to a bridge, fixed bayonets and thought they were going to have some 'fun', but nothing happened and so they settled down for the night. They advanced the next day through —— being resisted all the way and arriving there learned that the Germans had sent some of their men away by train. The streets were lined by delighted French people and the 'Sets' interpreter was embraced several times.
(*Corporals Bailey and Barrett, Chard and Ilminster News*)

17th October

Quiet day. 'A' Company was ordered to cross the river to Erquinghem to form a bridgehead. Remainder of battalion rested in billets. Stood to arms owing to a slight attack on 10th Brigade during night. Otherwise all quiet.

When it was light the villagers realised we were British and we were bombarded with jugs of hot coffee and bread and butter which was very welcome. The house opposite my section kept us supplied with tea and bread and jam all the morning. At 12 noon we dug a trench to our front and finished it about 4.00 p.m. On duty with six men guarding two barricaded roads. When off duty we slept in a hairdresser's shop. The woman gave us plenty of bedding to sleep on. She told us of the cruel treatment she had from the Germans. Her wrists were black and blue where the Huns had mauled her. They took her husband away, but he managed to escape. They stole all the razors and other things.
(*A Cook*)

After lunch go on 'police duty' in village stopping refugees coming back in case some of them are spies, most unpleasant; stay there till 6.00 p.m. was given coffee etc.
(*Edward Packe*)

18th October

At 4.30 a.m got a sudden order to move at 6.30 a.m. to Nieppe. Order did not get to 'A', 'B' and 'H' Companies in time for them to get breakfast before starting. Battalion waited at cross roads in Nieppe until about 10.00 a.m, then cooked breakfast. Apparently the III Army Corps attacking the position east of Armentieres, which covered Lille and the Brigade, is in Corps Reserve. Brigade moved about 10.00 a.m into Armentieres. Somerset L I and Hants had dinners in station yard. Rifle Brigade and East Lancs went off to the left. About 4.00 p.m the Battalion was ordered to be ready to move to Epinette in support of an attack to be made by East Lancs and Rifle Brigade to help the 10th Brigade who were hung up. This attack was soon after cancelled and the Battalion went into billets in the railway station. This billet was very exposed to shellfire so an early start was decided upon.

> Then through Nieppe to Armentieres and halted for dinner outside the railway goods shed. Shells were falling in the town not far from us and there was heavy firing for several hours just to our front. Spent the night in the Railway Booking Office.
> (*A Cook*)

Chapter Seven

Action at Le Gheer
19th–27th October

19th October

Moved out of billets at 4.30 a.m. to a farm on Erquinghem road about 1000 yards west of railway station. Remained here until 5.00 p.m then moved about 1/2 mile to a factory on River Lys where got good cover. Quiet night.

20th October

Expected to remain in present billets for the night. C.O and Company commanders settled down to arrange promotions etc; but about 1.00 p.m. orders came to move at once to Pont de Nieppe. On arrival there at 3.00 p.m got orders direct from 4th Division to move to Ploegsteert and report to Colonel Anley, Commander 12th Brigade. He wanted the battalion to remain in reserve and we went into billets in Ploegsteert. Companies very scattered, down streets etc.

21st October

Ordered to be prepared to move at 1/4 hours notice during night, but did not have to turn out. Eventually ordered to move at 4.30 a.m. No time to arrange breakfasts. Moved out to Point 63 (1 mile north of Ploegsteert). Much rain last night and coming very heavy. C.O. and Company Commanders ordered to reconnoiter towards Wolverghem. In their absence an order came for battalion at once to move to road junction near Chateau. Adjutant was senior officer left and Company commanders were all 2nd Lieutenants. Met General Hunter-Weston at this point and he issued orders for the battalion to counter attack against Le Gheer village which had been occupied at dawn by Germans who had driven out the Inniskilling Fusiliers. The loss of Le Gheer uncovered the flank of the line running about 200 yards east of the Bois de Ploegsteert, occupied by the Cavalry, who were thus enfiladed. They were, however, hanging on, though losing heavily. As the G.O.C. was issuing his orders the C.O., 2nd in command and Company commanders appeared. The Battalion was guided by a cavalry officer to St Yves, at northeast corner of Bois de Ploegsteert where orders were issued by C.O. for 'A' and 'B' to advance through eastern edge of wood and attack le Gheer cross roads and clear the village. 'C' and 'H' 'were kept in support. Battalion Headquarters were established in an Estaminet at Bois de Ploegsteert. At 10.50 a.m. 'A' Company reached Le Gheer cross roads with 'B' in support southeast corner of wood and a company of East Lancs lining south edge of wood.

At 11.45 a.m. 'A' was pushing through the village and 'B' Company was at cross roads. Each house was surrounded and then searched by two men. This was carried on systematically until the village was cleared at 12.55 p.m. The southern and eastern faces were held.

During the advance through the village 'A' Company captured 101 prisoners and released 2 officers and 40 men of the Inniskilling Fusiliers who had been made prisoners by the Germans in the morning.

Our company was ordered to proceed through a very thick wood and clear it of Germans. We advanced in extended order swept through the wood and, as far as I could see, my platoon seemed to be the only platoon in touch with our company commander. When we got half way through we were told to alter our direction so as to bring our men out on to the left corner of the wood as we found that the Huns had retired from the front wood and taken up a position in their trenches in front of the wood. After some difficulty we managed to get the other platoons up and then we got the order to advance against the village, and clear it of Huns. Captain (Yatman) then called for volunteers and he and four men rushed across the field and got under shelter of the first house, then I came across with about six men fully expecting to be plugged as we raced across the open or shot at by a machine gun from some house or other. We reached the house but found the Germans had pulled further back so we used this house as a base as went on to another house opposite but found the Huns had left that also. We then went on to the main part of the village, arranging that Captain (Yatman) should take the left half and I the other. I got my men up to some ricks which had been used as a German observation post and from these across the main road into a public house where I was joined by ———.

There we collected ourselves and I headed up our men then totalling four-teen. From there we got into a farm house on the way to which one of our men was hit in the forehead bringing our number down to the regimental number. Here we were sniped by some Germans in houses on our right. An extraordi-nary thing then happened to one of our men who was running across the field to join us. A shot rang out behind us followed by several others and this man's coat was seen to burst into flames and I have never seen anyone get rid of his clothes quicker. It turned out that he had passed a trench of Huns on the left and they had hit this man in one of his ammunition pockets, which had

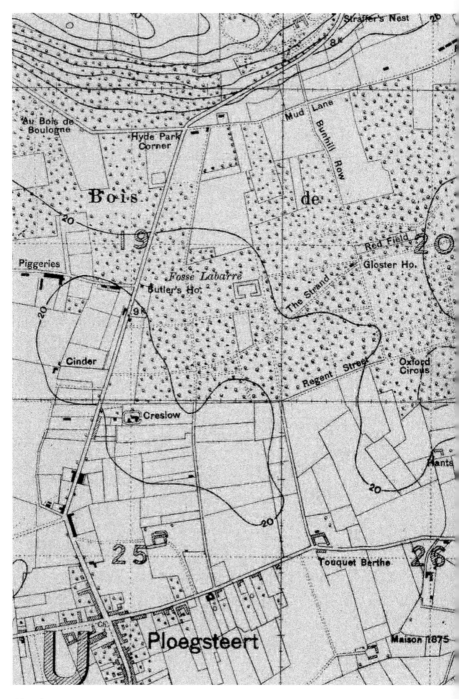

Map 6
Ploegsteert (Trench map)

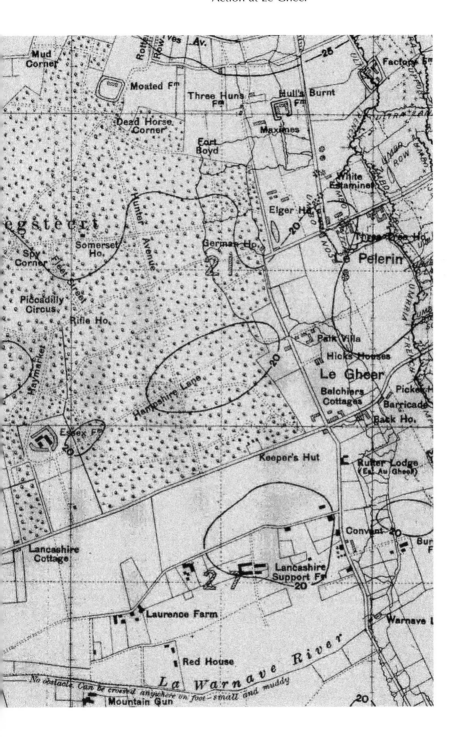

Figure 5
Ploegsteert. (*Somerset Light Infantry Archive*)

exploded giving him a nasty burn on his side. We fired on them through the windows and succeeded in killing one and hitting another. They gave us a very small target as they used to bob up round the corner and fire and then down again. ——— shot one with his revolver, a very good shot. Some of us then crossed to another farm and joined ———. A German was seen lying in a ditch a little to our right so we went across with some five men to get him. And then a wonderful thing happened from out of the other trench in a mangel field rose up 42 Germans and with one exception all threw down their arms and surrendered. They had been in the trenches a long time and were very hungry. Then the house was taken and we captured 21 more prisoners and in addition rescued two sections of the Inniskilling Regiment with three officers, who had been confined in the cellars by the Huns. These men were very glad to get away but said that the Huns had treated them kindly.

We bowled over a good many of the enemy from the house and then we raced on to a hedge. ——— taking his men to the right while I cut a hole in the hedge and tumbled our men through and made for the next fence as the last was too hot to stay at. Private ———, a splendid servant of Captain ——— was killed and soon afterwards Lieutenant ——— was shot in the hand and went back to hospital. I was awfully sorry to see him go, as he had been a great friend of mine out here. We took our final position here, capturing 25 Germans before they could get away. Several more gave themselves up making the total of ninety odd captured. We drove out of the village altogether about 600 Huns.

I was unfortunate enough to lose two sergeants; one of them had been awarded the Medal Militaire, a great honour much coveted by French soldiers. (*Unnamed Officer, Somerset County Gazette*)

My Company 'A' led the attack, the other companies being in reserve. We advanced to the far edge of Ploegsteert Wood, fixed bayonets and rushed the nearest house, but found it empty. We began pouring heavy machine gun fire into it and into the back of the house we were in. We moved round to the front as the bullets were coming through the windows and walls. Several fowls in the road outside were knocked over. We then advanced to the other houses and surrounded one of which was full of Germans and captured twenty. Another party threw down their arms and surrendered to only seven of us. Yet another party of 15 surrendered to a Corporal of my Company! He had his hands full till he could get rid of them. There was one house flying the Red Cross flag which was occupied by 20 Germans and a machine gun. They gave us trouble at first but we eventually overcame their resistance and captured them. One of

Figure 6
La Gheer. (*Somerset Light Infantry Archive*)

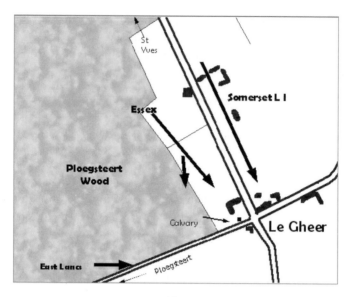

Map 7
Attack on La Gheer, October 21st 1914

my men out of curiosity went down to the cellar and to his surprise found
about 40 British prisoners from the Inniskillings under a German armed
guard. The latter hastily threw down their arms. The Inniskillings were grateful at being released. We took all our objectives with few casualties. We later
took up a position on the far side of the village. There had been a continuous
roar of guns and rifles which made us slightly deaf. Our men had great fun
today as they stood up hour after hour shooting at the enemy. Our captures
were about 100 and about 400 dead and wounded Boche were reported in the
vicinity. Shortly afterwards we were relieved by the East Lancs. and went back
to the village of St. Yves where we had a good sleep. I slept on a heap of pota-
toes, but was too tired to notice how uncomfortable the feathers were.
(*Arthur Coo*k)

With my Company 'A' consisting at the time of about 200 men, we advanced
through the village, and before the fighting was over had accounted for over
400 dead and 126 prisoners. We had the advantage over the Germans, as they
were retiring, and we were firing at them all the time from the tops of hayricks,
windows of houses, etc. I could only account for six casualties in my own platoon. When they were about 100 yards outside the village the Germans took
up a final position in the trenches that had been lost by the Inniskillings. Then
we charged and took the trenches with the bayonet, accounting for a good
many of the enemy in that way. In the vicinity of Le Gheer our Battalion
accounted altogether for 1400 killed and wounded. We managed to take the

village ourselves although there were other Companies to our right and left. The enemy consisted entirely of Saxons and they were much superior as far as numbers were concerned. During the taking of Le Gheer by the Somersets we released from the cellars of one of the big houses some 50 N.C.O.s and Privates of the Inniskillings who the Germans had imprisoned but were unable to take away. Their imprisonment was pretty short for they were taken in the morning and released in the afternoon. During the attack on the trenches I advanced my platoon too quickly for the artillery behind us which began to shell us accidentally. We at once retired to some high ground about 100 yards in the rear – where we could cover the trenches with rifle fire – and send back information to the artillery of what was happening. We had nothing to eat that day and I remember that a Lance Corporal of my platoon crawled out to where two dead Germans were lying and got their rations, consisting of bread and bully beef. Some of us then sat down and enjoyed a meal. The Lance Corporal in question was also trying on the boots belonging to the dead Germans as his own were worn out.

(*Sergeant C Willcox – Awarded D.C.M. for this action*)

They also put up the white flag but we would not be taken in as we had some of it before. They put up the white flag and when our men go to take them prisoner they fire on them. So you can make sure we did not take any notice of it now.

(*T Lewis, Somerset County Gazette*)

During the fight, one trench full of Germans in the wood put up the white flag. We took no notice but shot it down three times. This so exasperated the Germans that they ran out of the trench, without their arms with their hands above their heads. It was with greatest difficulty that they could be persuaded to put them down.

(*G Prideaux*)

Then without warning, a trickle of sweating, cursing but quite good-tempered lads came through the woods behind us. They seemed to know what was expected of them, for at edge of the wood and without pausing, they fixed bayonets and, as one of our men said, vulgarly, went through the village of Le Gheer and the Boche occupiers 'like a dose of salts'. Presently a stream of wounded men began to trickle back to the cover of the woods. A man bearing on his back a wounded comrade, a young officer with a painful wound through the forearm, and another with a smashed finger, both of whom refused to be dressed until their men were seen to. One poor fellow seemed to have stopped half a dozen fragments of shrapnel with his face; another had been caught by a burst of machine gun bullets. They moaned pitifully until the ambulance man gave them a shot of something in the arm. The edge of the wood became an advanced dressing station. It looked like a slaughterhouse. Meanwhile, in the village the Hun was having a rough time. He was quite unprepared for an

attack from this side, and the Somerset lads were in the main street before the
Germans were aware of the danger. Trench after trench was taken, the British
bayonets doing savage work that hot evening. Heaps of Germans filled the
dugouts on the edge of the village, and when we got to the far side the enemy
was on the run.

(*Lieutenant Colonel N.G. Thwaites 4th Dragoon Guards, 'A Walk around Plugstreet'.*)

As soon as the Somersets had captured the village and cut off the retreat of the
Germans, some Inniskilling Fusiliers advanced from the west, and the East Lancs
charged out of the wood to the south. The enemy was completely bewildered
and ran about in all directions, during which more prisoners were captured.
(*History*)

From:	**G.O.C 11th Brigade**
To:	**Somerset Light Infantry**
Time:	**1217**

Well done. I can always be sure that a task allotted to you will be well carried out. GOC 2nd
Cavalry Division wishes me to express to you his appreciation of the way in which you have
relieved a dangerous situation on his right. Good old Somersets. Signed A Hunter Wilson

---

At 1.20 p.m. a strong counter attack developed from the south and southeast against
le Gheer. O.C. 'A' Company reported he might have to retire to edge of Bois de
Ploegsteert and needed reinforcements. Adjutant went off to see G.O.C. at Brigade
HQ, but there were no more reinforcements. Two Platoons of 'C' Company were
sent up to 'A' Company's position. 'H' and 'C' Companies (less 2 platoons) were
retained at Battalion H.Q. to deal with a possible attack, which was threatened from
the east. 'A' Company however held it's ground. At 5.15 p.m. orders were received for
11th Brigade to take over line held by 12th Brigade and 2nd Cavalry Brigade.
Somerset L I to hold line from village of Le Gheer to village of St Yves). This could
not be done until after dark as the companies at Le Gheer were in action and could
not be relieved until nightfall. This line was taken over by 'C' and 'H' Companies
from 2nd Cavalry Brigade about 6.30 p.m. Battalion Headquarters remained at same
place. 'A' and 'B' Companies moved into billets at St Yves. Quiet night. Casualties 1
Officer, Lt Vincent wounded, 7 men killed, 19 wounded.

When I took my boots off in the cottage I found that the abscess on the
instep of my foot had burst and the foot was now quite comfortable after being
very painful for days. I'd quite forgotten the foot during the excitement and
fright of the attack.

We made this attack in Full Marching Order with fifty extra rounds of
ammunition and in greatcoats sodden with rain.

(*Edward Packe*)

On the 20th October advanced posts of the 12th Brigade of the 4th Division, III Corps, were forced to retire, and at dusk it was evident that the Germans were likely to make a determined attack. This ended in the occupation of Le Gheer by the enemy.

As the position of the Cavalry at St. Yves was thus endangered, a counter-attack was decided upon and planned by General Hunter-Weston and Lieutenant-Colonel Anley. This proved entirely successful, the Germans being driven back with great loss and the abandoned trenches reoccupied. Two hundred prisoners were taken and about forty of our prisoners released.
(*Official Despatches*)

22nd October

'A' and 'B' Companies were ordered to move near Chateau at Point 63 in reserve. Battalion Headquarters moved up to an Estaminet in St Yves about 6.00 a.m. At about 10.00 a.m. the village of St Yves was heavily shelled. The Battalion Headquarters Estaminet was destroyed almost at once. Fortunately the officers and men were outside and none were hurt. Headquarters moved to a cellar in another house. During the afternoon a terrific shellfire was poured into St Yves. Bombproofs had been constructed during the night and everyone got into them. The house selected as Battalion Headquarters was hit several times. The officers had left the cellar fortunately and were under a wood stack. About 2.00 p.m. orders were received for 'A' and 'B' Companies to take over the line from St Yves to River Douve at present held by Hants. This they did after dark. The Battalion is now all in the front line in trenches dug by the Cavalry with Battalion Headquarters in a house at St Yves. During the night the Estaminet in the Bois de Ploegsteert was destroyed by shellfire. Quiet night.

> Deuce of a noise at Le Gheer about 4.30, had to go down there. 'C' and 'H' Companies holding trenches behind Messines, don't know quite what for. About 2.30 p.m. was told to reconnoitre trenches held by Hampshires near river Douve. Took a long time. I had time for a small snatch of food, then collected the company and took over about 8.00 p.m. Rotten trenches and rotten place. Heavy firing somewhere and a good many shots over us, no one hurt.
> (*F S Bradshaw*)

> Many houses have been hit in the vicinity and houses and ricks set on fire, places only vacated a few hours ago by peaceful inhabitants. Birds were singing in their cages, pigs grunting for food in the styes, horses neighing in the stables for fodder, the remains of meals on tables and hot embers still in the grates. We moved off at 5.00 p.m. and relieved the Hampshires holding a line of trenches at the top end of the village of St. Yves, between Messines and Ploegsteert Wood.
> There's a lot of noise and firing at 9.45 p.m. to 10.30 p.m. but no damage done except the barrel of my rifle which I appear to have fired with the plug

of four by two in the barrel, to keep out the rain, still there.
(*Edward Packe*)

23rd October

Companies improved their trenches during night and a bombproof was dug for
Battalion Headquarters near present house. No shelling today to speak of. Heavy
firing during the night but no actual attack.

Went round at about 6.30 a.m. quite quiet. Had a snack at breakfast then
trekked about all day. My company occupied about 1000 yards, so I had a great
deal of walking. Water is hard to get. Got down for a rest at 4.15 p.m. but at
4.45 p.m. cavalry officer came in to discuss the situation, he didn't like it but
nothing could be done. Lots of firing during the night and did not get sleep
until 5.00 a.m. Glossop hit in the leg, not very bad.
(*F S Bradshaw*)

We worked on the trenches all last evening and night trying to get them into
good defensive order. There was a slight attack but a few bursts of rifle fire settled that. I passed the house where I slept last night and those occupied by
other troops in St. Yves. They were shelled to the ground and burning. We
were shelled a good bit today but our trench is now fairly deep but safe by
keeping at the bottom of it. Some shells fell very near and gave us a good
sprinkling of dirt, which is unpleasant if you have the tea laid. The road running along behind our trench leads to Messines. In front of us about 1,000
yards away is a road running parallel with our trench and during the day the
enemy use it occasionally.
    Today we had great fun sniping at a horseman, then at a cyclist and two
walking on foot. I think that was why we got shelled. I will leave them alone
tomorrow in case Fritz gets angry and starts throwing souvenirs at us. We were
attacked in the night but easily held our own.
(*Arthur Cook*)

There were four or five farmhouses all standing in a row in close proximity and
a few yards in front of the line of buildings was a trench occupied by the
Somersets. Parallel to this trench the nearest point occupied by the enemy was
a trench 650 yards away. And behind this about 200 yards ran another trench
also occupied by the enemy. The German artillery was far in the rear of their
trenches – a mile or two at any rate. With remarkable quickness and accuracy
the artillery had got the range of the British trenches, but first they made the
farmhouses their objective. So the shells soon hurtled through the air and soon
the farms were blazing. All the domestic part of the homestead with the
exception of the kitchen had been destroyed. It was between three o'clock and
four o'clock in the afternoon and me and my mate had gone into the

Map 8
Positions at Le Gheer 23rd October 1914. (*Somerset Light Infantry Archive*)

farmhouse to get some water to cook dinner for ourselves. It is always better
for two to muck in together. Off they went to the kitchen of the farmhouse
oblivious to the bursting shells to fetch some cold water. We had just come out
of the farmhouse with some water and were crossing between the barns when
I don't know exactly what happened. I heard a bang and then felt something
and the ground came up to meet me. When I came to my senses I said to my
bloke 'What's that?' All I could see was the blood spurting. He said 'some of
those snipers got you mate'.

Soon after I was hit General Hunter-Weston came up to me and patted me
on the shoulder saying 'Hard luck Corporal, jolly bad luck. Never mind you'll
get your own back some day' and off he went singing Ragtime. We soldiers out
here know him as the 'Ragtime General' for he is always singing Ragtime
songs. A fine polished one he is and there is no such thing as fear about him.
He goes about singing ragtime all the while and whenever you see him he has
a cheery smile on his face. 'Never mind' he once said 'if they (the Germans)

won't come for us then we'll go and get them and really give them 'Alexander's Ragtime Band.'

When I got shot I was carried back into Headquarters. I was handed over to the stretcher-bearers who carried me to a Maltese cart. Then I was taken in a motor ambulance and eventually on to the boat. From Southampton I went directly to Wandsworth. It was October 23rd when I got my wound and it was just three days afterwards that I reached the hospital. In the two days after I was wounded I did not see a doctor. It was on the boat that I first received attention from a doctor. He washed my wound bandaged me up and packed me up all right for travelling.

It was a rifle bullet that knocked me out I don't blame the German who fired it. It must have been a stray shot for the Germans are miserable shots with the rifle. They couldn't hit the town they came from. Anyhow that bullet found me, it took me just at the side of my left nostril, passed through my lip, struck out the teeth from that of that side of my mouth and then turned upwards into the palette. I remember spitting my teeth out but I swear there was no bullet among them.

(*Corporal Kelson, Bath Chronicle*)

24th October

Heavy sniping all day, but not much shelling. Remained in present positions.

As to our trenches, when we took them over they were square holes about 4 feet across and 4 feet deep with the earth chucked up for head cover and loopholes made with faggots covered with earth. In here two people lived. The first two days and nights all went well but on the third night it rained like mad and for my part I spent the rottenest and most miserable night out here. When I woke up I was, literally, sitting in water. This obviously wouldn't do, so while it was still early, we went across to the cottages and I and my pal secured two doors and two shutters. We dug out about another 2 feet backwards and covered the hole up with doors and shutters and then chucked the earth back on top. Thus not only having a rainproof house but also a partial shellproof house. We left a space of about 16" for egress across which at night we spread a waterproof sheet, which every man is supplied with. One door we put on the ground in our hole to lie on and we are very comfortable too. It may strike you as an awful shame to remove the doors and shutters from the cottages, but when you realise that the whole village had been set on fire by the shells and burnt and that they were shelling these cottages daily, it doesn't seem so bad. The first time we went into the cottage we found a dog, some goats, rabbits, canaries and a parrot all caged up. Seeing that these were in imminent peril of being burnt alive or starving, we ate the rabbits and loosed the dogs, the goats and canaries. The parrot, which could not fly, we took back to the trench with us and by day it used to sit on a perch outside and by night it slept in an empty ammunition box. When we were relieved we brought it along and gave it to a civilian who returned to her house back here. The goats never went far from the house and we used to get milk from them.

(*Edward Packe*)

Those who contribute sixpence to the have the satisfaction of knowing they are providing 1/7d worth of tobacco and cigarettes for our brave soldiers. Thanks to the cooperation of the War Office the packages of cigarettes and tobacco go post and duty free to the front. This remarkable success is the result of an appeal by the Gazette for funds, so that soldiers at the front should not be in want of tobacco while on active service. We hope that ever reader of the Gazette will spare as many sixpences as possible and swell the number of gifts sent to the front. For every sixpence forwarded, 10 English cigarettes and 4oz of tobacco of English manufacture will be sent to the front. On every parcel will appear the name and address of the donor whose money has paid for the packet. The Somersets will greatly appreciate this practical way of showing our immense admiration for the splendid manner in which they are upholding the County's honour.

Mr R. Mundy, 5 St Augustine, Taunton has very generously given a wire haired fox terrier to be auctioned for the fund and we are anxious to dispose of it to the highest bidder. It is valued at 30 shillings. What offers?

The French people have been very generous to Tommy but much as he appreciates the smokes they give him, he is unable to overcome his longing for the English cigarette he is always used to. He wants to be able to put his hand in his pocket and bring out a cigarette that he can smoke and enjoy. Just the ordinary English cigarette with the good old English flavour. He has been used to them since he started smoking and they are what he wants badly now. When we think of him in the trenches it will give some solace to know that his pockets are filled with what he wants just then. Long hours, long nights and often wet nights will not dampen his spirits if he can get his smoke. It's one thing that helps to keep hanging on.

Make your donation a weekly one, tobacco burns away so fill our soldiers pipes and keep them filled. So send a supply of cigarettes every week to keep him in smokes all the time he is away. That's why we want you to send your sixpence every week.

(*Somerset County Gazette*)

25th October

Fine morning. Usual sniping. Heavy bombardment of the village started about 3.00 p.m. 5 Houses burned, including 2nd Battalion H.Ops in St Yves, which was burned to the ground. Germans using incendiary napthene shells. Gunners have done good work yesterday and today in knocking down farms containing snipers and machine guns. Rained hard in evening and continued all night. Germans made attack during night and a few of them got up to within 400 yards of our trenches. Our trenches are absolute quagmires in this weather, causing extreme discomfort to men and filling the rifles with mud.

I went out just before dawn and set fire to a farm between ours and the enemy's lines where the enemy could mass for attack unseen. We now felt that we could hold the line against any attack but the ground being difficult to dig we had not got very good cover against shell fire. Our machine guns had done same useful work, especially at night, but owing to not having an alternative position, were one day knocked out by the enemy's guns. Shells pitched right on them, but only one man was killed. The enemy's guns had got the range perfectly, but we also experienced their first attempts at sniping by machine guns, wonderfully accurate.
(W Whittuck)

Fritz has been nasty today and made things warm for us. We cannot leave the trench without being sniped and much shelling. It was a wet, black and miserable night. We let off a few rounds during the night hoping some would find a good billet. There are four large fires burning which give away all our movements during the night to the enemy. Then they annoy us with machine gun fire. We put a trip wire in front of our trench. We are having fine feeds here off the cattle and poultry left behind. We found a pig wandering about and decided to kill it. No one seemed game to do the job, so at last we put him in a sack and shot him. We burned him off and divided him up. In the meantime we found a large pot and caught some fowls, rabbits and a goat and they all went into the pot together. It took a lot of cooking, for when Jerry started shelling we had to run for cover leaving the pot to carry on stewing by itself. The best of it was when Jerry just missed putting a shell right into the pot, which threw up a lot of dirt which settled in our stew. But we did not mind a bit of dirt! The stew was excellent – I had two or three helpings! We also nearly got a calf, it was wandering about behind us and one fellow said, 'Where's my rifle, I'll have a pot at him.' He had his pot at 50 yards, but the calf swished his tail, looked round as much as to say, 'Who done that' and wandered off into the German lines. We think it must have been a spy.
(Arthur Cook)

26th October

Quiet day. Usual shelling and sniping. No casualties.

Saxon sniping became very accurate, and it soon grew extremely unhealthy to walk about in open during the day. Both sides appear to have been rather jumpy and over-strained. Heavy firing broke out twice just at dawn, but no real

attacks took place. Enemy shelled us regularly at 2.00 p.m. every day for about an hour, but no great damage.
(*W Watson*)

From:	**11th Brigade**
To:	**Rifle Brigade, Hants, East Lancs, Somerset L.I**
Time:	**1344**

G.O.C. wishes to point out the necessity for control of fire in attacks, he has formed the opinion that last night there was an unnecessary amount of firing from our trenches. He wishes to stress on all ranks the extreme importance of having a sure target before opening fire.

Cleared up during the day. Plenty of sniping during the day. Lance Corporal Rose, looking through Glossop's glasses, got shot in the head, very bad luck, he will probably die.
(*F Bradshaw*)

More shells and sniping today. We had rare fun with Jerry when fetching our water, which we had to get from a well near a house about 50 yards behind us. If we want any during the day we have to rush across the open ground behind our trench. Jerry is always watching and starts sniping, but has no success at hitting a running man. You can bear his bullets striking behind you which gives you no cause for delay. He should practise aiming off! Our C.S.M. (Parker) was wounded in both legs by a shell. The night was fairly quiet but Messines, on our left, is being shelled heavily and many fires started.
(*Arthur Cook*)

27th October

Fine day. A welcome reinforcement of officers arrived today consisting of Captains Smith and Campbell and Lieutenants Watts and Orr.

Our platoon's trench was rather on the left of our line, to our right; about 100 yards away were two more of our platoons and another regiment. To our rear was a road about 35 yards away which ran parallel to the trenches and which was connected with another road about 200 yards off which led to a village.

Behind our trench there were three cottages just across the road and a shallow ditch ran from our trench to the road. To our front, first a ploughed field for 200 yards then a mangel field with 2 haystacks and 2 chicken huts in it with to the left a couple of barns. Beyond the haystacks, a dip, then a road at about 1000 yards, then the main German trenches on the horizon.

The Germans had small trenches in the mangel field connecting the huts and haystacks and barns and from here they used to snipe at us whenever we gave them chance. It was also from these trenches that they made their night attacks. Two of the three started when I was on sentry-go. Altogether they gave us three night attacks, but they were faint-hearted to the extreme and I don't believe they moved out of their trenches. The second lasted the longest for about 2½ hours but in spite of that I only fired 15 rounds because it is such a waste of ammunitions firing at a flash, so I waited at my loophole until I could see a German's body against the skyline, but they never appeared. Each time they started the attack by sending up a sort of rocket which burst high up and made the whole place as bright as day and then they started shooting. They shelled the village behind us beforehand so as to set the houses on fire and light our position up, and they did their best to burn the three cottages behind our trench but weren't successful, and although they hit them two or three times they didn't do much damage. We used to cook food and wash etc. in those cottages, which always provided a sort of triple amusement. First, getting out of the trench and running down the ditch crossing the road and getting in the cottage. Secondly the offchance of a shell or two to help cook the food and thirdly the return journey to the trench. The first day we were rather shy of them, but we found they were rotten bad shots and we got contemptuous and used to stop and wave our hands and blow kisses and make various rude gestures to them before setting off back again to the trenches. We only had one man out of our platoon slightly hit during the whole time we were there, although a good many shell burst in the road and on the cottage. When it got dusk and in the early morning we used to come out like rabbits and one morning were playing football with a child's ball we had found in one of the cottages and they turned a Maxim in our direction. The football stopped abruptly, but it was too misty for them to hit us and all got safely back to our trenches. Another evening we were standing chattering outside our trenches when they put over a volley of three shells, which burst about 20 to 30 yards to our right not doing any harm except to the Imperial purse.

The Germans only gave us decent target twice, on both of which occasions the 'lookout' took the greatest advantage and at any rate two Germans are out of action as a result of our stay there; it didn't fall to be my luck to be look-out on either occasion, but I had a pot at a motor car going along the far road 1000 yards off, but although we turned it back I don't suppose we did any damage. As to the night attacks, I don't suppose our bullets did any more damage than theirs and if there were any Germans dead in the morning they must have died of fright. (*Edward Packe*)

Lance Corporal W Williams, Privates Hansford and Croker were sent out to burn down a house in front of the trenches, which the enemy used for sniping. Private Croker was severely wounded and the party was cut off. The other two brought him in under heavy fire. They burnt the house. (*Lt Col C B Prowse*)

Chapter Eight

First Battle at Ypres
28th October–15th November

28th October

Were relieved today by Hants Regiment in our trenches and we moved back into reserve near Chateau north of Bois De Ploegsteert. Very fine day with bright moon at night. Rather a bad night for carrying out the relief. The following was the system of relieving adopted. Company commanders and platoon representatives of our companies met corresponding parties of Hants. Platoon representatives took Hants reps to their trenches and explained situation, targets etc. The Hants reps then brought up their platoons at short intervals and our platoon moved independently to company rendezvous and thence back to their new quarters. Headquarters at Estaminet on road south of Chateau. Started relieving about 7.00 p.m but did not get settled down till about 9.00 p.m. as the relieving took a long time.

> Black and white dog shot between the lines. Doble claims to have shot a couple of Huns otherwise quiet except for some sniping and one or two shells. The Hampshires relieved us at 6.30 p.m. and we spent a good night in a barn. (*Edward Packe*)

29th October

Quiet day in our neighbourhood but very heavy fighting north of Messines. The most peaceful day for a long time – fear it may the calm before the storm. Fears justified in the evening when a heavy attack was made on Le Gheer. It was beaten off by the East Lancs.

30th October

Very severe fighting today. An artillery bombardment of all the 11th Brigade

trenches from Warnave to Douve River commenced about 7.00 a.m and continued to 3.00 p.m. In morning, Adjutant sent to Le Gheer to East Lancs
Headquarters to make arrangements for the Battalion to take over their trenches
tonight. These Headquarters and the approaches were very dangerous. Owing to
the probability of a general attack following the bombardment the relief was cancelled for tonight. About midday messages came in from Hants at Le Gheer that
infantry were massing in front of them. About 3.30 p.m. they reported the situation is critical, infantry were advancing to within 30 yards and one platoon was
annihilated and its trenches destroyed by shellfire. G.O.C. sanctioned not more
than half a company from the battalion being sent to reinforce 'C' Company of
the Hants. Our 'C' and 'H' Companies had been sent to Ploegsteert about 2.00
p.m. As reserve to the right flank, we were recalled by General on his hearing of
the situation at St Yves. 2nd Lieutenant Braithwaite's platoon of 'A' Company
arrived in Hants trench just as enemy broke through the line where the platoon
had been wiped out. The trench was in a sunken road and this the enemy poured
across. A barricade was hastily erected and great slaughter inflicted on the enemy
by this platoon. At 4.45 p.m. the enemy were still pouring into the trench and
attacking the barricade. O.C. Hants considered the situation be critical and the
remainder of 'A' Company was accordingly sent up to the Hants at 5.15 p.m. At
5.30 p.m. Major Prowse went to confer with Colonel Parker (Hants) as the result
of a message from G.O.C. 11th Brigade suggesting a counterattack by night. No
more of our regiment were put into the trenches and about 6.00 p.m. the firing
died down. Major Prowse personally reconnoitered the position and located
Germans in the trench previously held by the lost platoon and in buildings in its
vicinity. He and Colonel Parker accordingly arranged that two companies of this
Battalion should surround the houses and trench and attack with the bayonet. 'C'
and 'H' Companies were detailed for this duty. 'A' and 'B' Companies held a line
behind the Hants trenches to support them. The Divisional Cyclist Company and
Divisional Squadron and one company Inniskilling Fusiliers were also sent up to
support Major Prowse. They were utilized to hold a third line.

On 30th October my Battalion was reserve battalion for the Brigade under
orders from the G.O.C.
   About midday messages were received from the Hants Regiment that the
enemy were massing on their front. A very heavy bombardment had been
poured on the trenches. At 3.30 p.m a message was intercepted to G.O.C 11th
Brigade from O.C. Hants, stating that the situation was critical, one platoon
annihilated and its trenches destroyed by shellfire and asking for urgent reinforcements. I passed this on to the G.O.C. On my own decision, sent a platoon
under 2nd Lieutenant Braithwaite and Sergeant Wilcox to reinforce the Hants,
with another platoon ready to start. I shortly received an order from the
G.O.C, 11th Brigade that I could reinforce up to two platoons.
   About dark I received a message from Lieutenant Braithwaite stating that
the enemy had broken through and asking for reinforcements. I turned out my
Battalion, drew an inner line behind the Hants with two companies and sent

out patrols to locate the enemy, who, I found had pierced the line on the Hants left centre and were occupying some houses and an estaminet in and behind the lines. I reconnoitered this position with my officers and taking one company to form a new garrison for the lost trenches, sent another to recapture the trenches and houses with the bayonet. The other two companies still holding the inner line above mentioned. I found that Lieutenant Braithwaite's platoon had arrived at a critical time, had thrown a barricade across the road where the enemy had broken through and had pinned him down and prevented his further movement. The enemy was lying down within 50 yards, unable to move. The houses and estaminet were cleared and found evacuated with the exception of dead and wounded and the line reestablished.

The trench of the Hants that had been rushed had been occupied by a platoon whose strength had been reduced to ten men out of about 50. These men fought it out and only one man I understand returned, the remainder being killed and wounded. The R.E. informed later that 74 dead Germans were lying on and around the barbed wire of the trench.

(Sergeant C Wilcox was ordered to take his platoon to reinforce a regiment whose line had been broken by the enemy. He flung a barricade across the road pinned the enemy down with bayonet and rifle fire and prevented them from moving until reinforcements came up. This N.C.O. has repeatedly been mentioned for gallantry in the war and has since been invalided, severely wounded.) (*Lt Col C B Prowse*)

I was ordered to take my platoon to reinforce the platoons of the Hants Regiment that were left. I got up there with only about forty men, and I could see it was rather a dangerous job. We could hear shouts coming from our left, 'Hands up! Hands up!' That cry continued for nearly two hours, and we didn't know whether it was coming from our men or the Germans. The suspense nearly drove us mad, and it was much worse than being fired at. I thought matters looked very suspicious, and with picks and shovels we soon built a barricade across the road in case the Germans suddenly attacked. Just as we finished we could see a great mass advancing up the road towards us. When they came up to within fifty yards we shouted to them to halt. A reply came, 'Don't shoot. We are Grenadier Guards.' I knew very well that there were no Grenadier Guards within miles of us, but allowed them to advance up to within ten yards of our barricade. Then we opened fire, and at this close range managed to account for 200 dead. The Germans however, had managed to get a lot of men behind us as well. We sent back messages to say that we were practically surrounded and a couple of scouts were sent from the remainder of the Regiment to find out what was wrong. On seeing the scouts the Germans seemed to get the idea that the whole Battalion was about to advance. They retired from the rear of my platoon and returned to the front, as they were afraid of being cut off. That gave me a better chance to hold the position, as I only had one front to defend. I think we must have shot their officer, for they suddenly retired without a word. I must say, though, that when that huge mass

of men came up to within ten yards of us our hearts were in our mouths.
(*Sergeant C Wilcox*)

On the evening of the 30th the line of the 11th Infantry Brigade in the neighbourhood of St. Yves was broken. A counter-attack carried out by Major
Prowse with the Somerset Light Infantry restored the situation. For his services on this occasion this officer was recommended for special award.
(*Sir John French's despatches*)

German artillery very active today. One shell just missed our billet and made a
tremendous hole. These shells make a terrible droning noise coming through the
air. The Hampshires have sent down for reinforcements to come up and my platoon is ordered to go. Early in the afternoon we advanced under as much cover
as possible. On reaching Hants. Headquarters they were obviously excited and
one officer said, "I'm afraid you will never get up there." My platoon officer, Mr.
Braithwaite, laughed at the idea and said "Come on boys." We followed and
arrived not a moment too soon. "Thank God for the Somersets," they shouted.
The Hampshires had had a gruelling time, whole platoons having been blown out
of the trenches, which they had taken over from us only two days before. The
Germans had broken through our lines on the left and were coming up the road
to enfilade us. There was a rough barricade of a cart across the road. I got my
section behind it and opened rapid fire. It was now pitch dark and we could not
see the advancing enemy who were shouting, blowing whistles and making a devil
of a noise. I and another chap stood up behind the cart firing as hard as we could.
All at once I heard a moan from him and just caught him as he fell. A bullet had
passed just above his heart, so I bandaged him up and got him into shelter and,
later improvised a stretcher out of a door and got two men to carry him back.
The Germans continued to advance right on to our bayonets, but a lucky shot
from someone killed the leader. As soon as he fell they turned and fled leaving
many dead and wounded in the road. Our stretcher-bearers went out and collected the wounded. The Hants were very pleased with the show our platoon put
up and told us we had saved the whole line. They had suffered a terrific bombardment by a shell known as a 'Jack Johnson' which makes a crater nine to ten
feet deep and about 15 yards in diameter. The road we came up this afternoon
was blown to pieces by several direct hits from these shells. When the Germans
retreated we began to dig fresh trenches as the old ones were completely
destroyed. We finished this by midnight and were relieved by 'C' Company about
3.30 a.m. Major Prowse was very pleased with the show we had put up.
(*Arthur Cook*)

I am pleased to say I am in the best of health. We are having a very warm time
of it here, never mind, we are sticking it all right and having the best of it,
although we have lost a few men and a lot of officers. It is awful to see the dead
Germans lying about, but they can't help having so many killed as they come
on in such big masses and our quick firing soon stops them. It was awful the

other night when they tried to break through our lines; you see the dead and wounded they left behind. They came within twenty yards of us before they stopped. So it will tell you what it must have been like for them.
(*Private T F Lewis, Somerset County Gazette*)

31st October

At 12.30 a.m. 'C' and 'H' moved from their quarters to a spot about 400 yards in rear of buildings. The C.O took forward all officers carefully explained his plan. He ordered 'H' Company to detail parties to surround each locality and 'C' Company to be ready to occupy the trenches when they were cleared. Then, split up into small parties, each given a definite locality, 'H' Company moved forward to the attack. One by one the buildings were surrounded and searched, but no Germans were found in any of them. They must have left quite recently. Major Prowse had tried to get a field gun to blow the houses down but this could not be provided. By 3.30 a.m. the situation was restored. 'C' Company immediately moved into the trench previously held by 'C' Company of the Hants. Many German dead were found and one of trenches was full of the dead of No 10 Platoon Hants Regiment, of which there was only one survivor. Neither company sustained any casualty. The other three companies then returned to quarters at 4.00 a.m. A warm night.

During the day, Colonel Butler, Lancs Fusiliers came up to take over command of the section of defences from Le Gheer to Douve River. During the night Messines had been evacuated by us, but was retaken during the afternoon by the K.O.S.B.'s and K.O.Y.L.I. of the 9th Brigade. 'C' Company had had a very bad time and suffered heavily. During the afternoon Captain Jones-Mortimer and Captain Smith were wounded by high explosive shell. Lieut. Bradshaw was left in command of 'A' Company and 2/Lt. Chichester in charge of 'B'. These two companies were now on the line, Bridge, Douve River-Chateau-Messines Road-St. Yves. 'B' Company dug fire trenches during the night at the end of this line near St. Yves. Lance-Cpl. F. Newberry was awarded the D.C.M. for gallantry during the 31st. During the night Germans got into a trench about 600 yards north St Yves. Two sections of 'B' Company were lent to O.C. Hants regiment to recapture it. The counterattack failed with heavy casualties.

At daylight this trench was found to have been evacuated by the Germans and the line was restored.

From:	11th Brigade
To:	**Somerset Light Infantry**
Time:	**0414**

Hampshires report left trench of left centre company taken by Germans and that Lieutenant Twining tried to take it with two sections formed from Somersets but has failed. Germans are also being re-enforced. Deal with that situation using Somersets, Inniskilling Fusiliers and Lancs Fusiliers as you think desirable. I am moving up company Lancs Fusiliers to your Headquarters at once.

To:	**Somerset Light Infantry**
From:	**11th Brigade**
Time:	**0430**

Hampshires lost the left trench of the left centre company near the road and borrowed 2 sections from me to assist to retake it from the next trench to the south. This failed and my men practically wiped out. Sole survivor who returned, a reliable man, states large number of enemy there and re-enforcements coming up. If an attack is made very heavy losses will be incurred as no cover and enemy can bring fire from three sides. Suggest withdrawing men from neighbouring trench south temporarily and shelling them out with guns and maxims and then re-occupying trenches. You BMI just received, an attack across the open will incur heavy loss.

From:	**11th Brigade**
To:	**Somerset Light Infantry**
Time:	**0445**

Have told artillery point 63 that trench at road junction about 1/4 mile NNE of ST YVES has been taken by Germans and have asked him to open fire to prevent re-enforcements coming up. He could not open fire on trench itself with safety, as it is middle of your lines. The Germans should be counter-attacked at once with the bayonet and prevented moving southwest. Utilise company of Somersets and half company Hampshires that you have immediately under your hand and get Inniskilling Company and Lancs Fusiliers concentrated for action as you may think desirable. Of course do not use up all he reserves unnecessarily as Point 63 must be safeguarded.

From:	**11th Brigade**
To:	**Somerset Light Infantry**
Time:	**0455**

Your SL2 received. General is coming up to your Headquarters at once in car. Artillery have been told to open fire. Concentrate Inniskillings and Lancs Fusiliers companies. The trench must be retaken.

From:	**11th Brigade**
To:	**Point 63**
Time:	**0610**

The enemy been seen on the road junction North of ST YVES. It is essential that you should bring all guns you can to bear on this area at once as I expect a heavy attack through the gap they have made in our line.

On the 31st October I was out superintending night entrenching with Lieutenant Colonel Parker, commanding the Hants Regiment. At 11.00 p.m. an officer of the Hants reported that one of his trenches was being occupied by the enemy and asked for help to retake it, at the same time stating that he thought it was very weakly garrisoned and that probably only 3 or 4 Germans were in it.

He took 2 sections of my 'B' Company and with his own men went off to reoccupy the trench. About 1.30 a.m a Lance Corporal of one of my sections that had gone out came in wounded and reported that they had charged the trench, found a large number of the enemy in and around it and strong bodies of the enemy in the rear of it, that my two sections were practically wiped out. He also said that two of them had got to the trench and had pulled out two of the enemy, one of whom they shot and brought the other in as a prisoner.

I reported the situation to the G.O.C. 11th Brigade in conjunction with Lieutenant Colonel Parker and after consultation it was decided to retake the trench and restore the line at once. Owing, however, to the short period before daylight it was then 4.30 a.m. it was deemed impossible to carry out the above plan as the ground was absolutely open and without cover and also liable to cross and enfilade fire.

At dawn the enemy had withdrawn and the trench was reoccupied by the Hants Regiment

(*Lt Col C B Prowse*)

We expected that we should get a good grueling next day (31st) and we did. The beauties of dawn have never appealed to me; on this particular occasion they were particularly unattractive. Dead Saxons were lying close to the front of the trenches and some were actually on the road behind the support's dugouts. This particular section was considered the worst in the line. It was situated on high ground, the possession of which would dominate the village of St. Yves and the Ploegsteert Wood and was, consequently, a particular objective of the enemy's heavy artillery, variety known as 'Jack Johnsons' and 'Coal-boxes.' At the moment 'C' Company occupied these trenches they possessed the following grave disadvantages from a defensive point of view. Three platoons only could be accommodated in continuous line; one platoon on the left was isolated by 150 yards from the right of the next group of trenches, held by a company of the Hampshire Regiment. This isolated trench, capable of holding one platoon, had been captured the evening before 'C' Company took it over. No. 1 Platoon, under 2/Lieut. C. C. Ford, occupied this isolated trench at 5.00 a.m. From 7.30 a.m. until dusk the whole line of trenches underwent a heavy shellfire. At about 8.00 p.m. the enemy's infantry advanced in skirmishing order, making short rushes on the most approved Aldershot pattern. 'Charles' (2/Lieut. Ford) sent for reinforcements. An inspection of his trench showed that it was not feasible to place more men there. He has already suffered considerable losses. Two sergeants – Sgt. Iliffe and Sgt. Chapman – had been badly wounded. Two machine guns and two sections were available in reserve. These were moved out and placed in a convenient ditch and so fill the gap between

'Charles' and the right of the Hampshire Regiment. This has the desired effect. Machine gun firing diagonally across front. Saxon attack withered away. 'H' Company relieved 'C' Company about 9.00p.m., who retire to shelter in a corner of Ploegsteert Wood.
(*Unnamed Diary, History*)

Moved out at 10.00 a.m. and go in support of the Inniskillings, we lined the ditch of the road to Messines and had one or two Jack Johnsons over. Moved away from the road and went up to another barn and stayed there till things quietened down at about 9.30 p.m. then marched back to our own barn and slept like the dead.
(*Edward Packe*)

From:	14th Division
To:	11th Brigade
Time:	2047

Major Prowse, Somerset Light Infantry (God bless them) have restored the situation on my left. My line is now intact but the trenches are so blown to bits that they require re-digging during the night. This, Major Prowse has arranged to do with two reliefs of Somersets and I am confident we shall be as strong as ever tomorrow morning. Major Prowse is an officer of exceptional military ability and I recommend him for immediate promotion to Lieutenant Colonel. It was due to his excellent arrangements made by him on 21st that our counter attack on Le Gheer was so successful.

| From: | A Hunter Weston |
| To: | Major Prowse |

I congratulate you and your battalion on the dispositions you have made in our lines. Whenever I entrust you with a mission I never have any doubts as to the success of its issue. As recognition of your services and as a complement to a grand battalion that you have the honour to command I have recommended you for immediate promotion to Lieutenant Colonel

From:	4th Division
To:	11th Brigade
Time:	2132

G.O.C. wishes his heartiest congratulations conveyed to Hants for line defence and to the Somerset Light Infantry for their work this evening. He strongly endorses your recommendation regarding Major Prowse in a message just forwarded to III Corps.

1st November

Colonel Butler decided today to readjust the line as news was received of the fall of Messines. During last night Lieutenant Bush's platoon of 'A' Company was sent to reinforce Hants left Company on River Douve. Lieutenant Bush was wounded. 'B' Company's trenches dug last night were heavily shelled about noon and Lieutenant Chichester was buried under the parapet of his trench and was dug out only jut in time by Lieutenant Waddy, the Medical Officer who happened to be in the trench at the time. Another man who was buried at the same time died of suffocation. 'H' Company was heavily shelled during the afternoon. Lieutenant Montgomery was wounded, four men were killed and twelve wounded in their trench, and they held on to it with great difficulty. At dusk a company of the Lancs Fusiliers dug fresh trenches facing northeast. These were completed about midnight and were occupied by 'A' Company. 'C' Company dug itself in around the farm 500 yards north of the St Yves. The Hants held the line from St Yves-Le Gheer on the right of 'H' Company. Inniskilling Fusiliers held from 'C' Company's farm to River Douve on west of Ploegsteert-Messines road. 'B' Company was in reserve near St. Yves. Battalion Headquarters remained at Estaminet, as the Hants were still occupying the Headquarters of the line allocated to us.

2nd November

The position held by the Somersets faced east, northeast and north, and was therefore open to enfilade fire. Companies held the positions taken up during the night. 'H' Company again suffered very severely and 'A' Company also. Lieutenant Braithwaite was injured. One of 'H' Company's trenches and two of 'A' Company's were enfiladed by guns firing heavy shell from the east. There was little firing from the north in the direction from which the fresh attack was expected. Headquarters still remained near the Chateau. In the evening the Worcesters and Dorsets arrived. The Lancs Fusiliers relieved the Battalion at 6.30 p.m. and the Worcesters relieved the Hants. Both this battalion and the Hants suffered very heavily today. The battalion moved to the wood on the southern slopes of Point 63 about 9.00 p.m.

Six officers (including Major Prowse, who was promoted to the rank of Lieutenant Colonel), five N.C.O.'s and two privates were mentioned in despatches for their distinguished conduct during these actions.

> At 4.00 a.m. took over some bad trenches made by Lancashires. Badly shelled and lots of rifle fire. Hit through thumb about 7.00 p.m. About 2.00 a.m. went down to dressing station, was taken to Ballieul Hospital, stayed there the night.
> (F S Bradshaw)

Promoted Corporal. Another day of Hell under the continual hail of shells

and bullets. Why have we no artillery to retaliate? Men are being buried alive and blown to pieces all around me. Perhaps death is preferable to this infernal life. The Germans have made tremendous efforts to push us back but have failed up to now. Relieved in evening by the Lancs Fusiliers and went back to a wood on the west side of the Chateau and had a good sleep – the best for days.
(*Arthur Cook*)

Private Driscoll was wounded on November 2nd, the day they evacuated the advanced trenches under cover of darkness and proceeded to make the reserve trenches more tenable. This work ceased a daybreak and later after breakfast the men were sitting in trench, chatting and smoking. As a protection against shell splinters the trench contained an improvised roof. Driscoll was seated behind a door when with out warning a shell weighing 18lb fell upon the structure and exploded. He was buried beneath the debris and unconscious for about an hour. At first he was thought to be dead but on showing signs of life, his head, which was bleeding profusely, was bandaged by a comrade. The shell also wounded five other men, two on one side of him and three on the other. Private Driscoll would have undoubtedly been killed

Figure 7
St. Yves. (*Somerset Light Infantry Archive*)

Figure 8
Burning farms, St. Yves. (*Somerset Light Infantry Archive*)

but for the head covering. That morning no less than four officers were
wounded. Viz Captain Jones Mortimer, Lieutenants Bush, Chichester and
Bradshaw.

Private Driscoll told how he had lain in the trench until 6.30 p.m. when he
managed to crawl to the base where his wound was thoroughly dressed. Later
he was attended at a field hospital and sent on a Red Cross train to Boulogne
and thence on the hospital ship Asturias to Southampton where he arrived on
November 5th. There were 1,400 on board and two died during the crossing
which fortunately was a smooth one
(*Somerset County Gazette*)

Moved out to another trench facing North towards Messines to guard the
flank of the Battalion, this meant we get enfiladed by the Germans. An
unpleasant day, almost as bad as Ligny. Joe Stead got hit in the back by a
shrapnel bullet as he was bending down in the trench to do up his bootlace.
How the shrapnel missed me I don't know because I was standing on top of
the trench, in a direct line and between Joe and the shrapnel burst. Frank
Bradshaw also wounded but only slightly. Stood to Arms at 5.15 p.m. as an
attack is expected and continued under Arms till we are relieved at 8.30 p.m.

Moved back to wood and cooked bacon and tea.
(*Edward Packe*)

3rd November

The bivouac was heavily shelled in the morning, and the Battalion moved to another position about 300 yards south of Point 63 and spent a quiet day and night. Orders were received about 2.00 p.m. for the Battalion to relieve the East Lancs at Le Gheer but this was afterwards cancelled. Blankets were drawn tonight but had to repacked about 10.00 p.m. owing to the Battalion being ordered to stand by owing to a threatened attack from Messines against Point 63. Major Elgar and Captain Allfrey joined the battalion today. Major Elgar took over duties of Senior Major, Captain Yatman going back to command 'H' Company, Captain Campbell 'B' Company, and 2nd Lieutenant Denny remained in 'B' Company. Lt Whittock returned to 'H' Company. Lieutenant Prideaux (Transport Officer) attached to 'A' Company for duty owing to shortage of officers.

4th November

Raw November day. We expected to go into the trenches tonight but are not ordered to after all. Four parties of women digging a 2nd line of trenches during afternoon. A very wet night. Very wretched for the men sleeping out of doors in a wet wood. Many men sick with rheumatism.

5th November

Fine warm day. Bivouac heavily shelled twice during the day. In the evening one man was killed and three wounded in 'A' Company by a shrapnel shell. The guns are placed along the southern slope of Point 63 and presumably the shells were meant for them. 2nd Lieutenant Braithwaite went sick today with a chill. We were ordered to relieve the Lancs Fusiliers in the trenches tonight but the order was cancelled almost immediately as the Battalion was required to support a projected French attack on Messines. 'C' Company under Captain Watson preceded by a patrol of three sections under Lieutenant Ford was sent out to get in touch with the French right at La Plus Douve Farm and to follow up the attack. Just as this company was starting (about 7.32 p.m.) a report came from the Dorsets on northern slopes of Point 63 to say Germans had penetrated their line on the Messines-Ploegsteert road. Major Prowse at once sent up a company to their support (8.00 p.m.) and reported to Colonel Butler, commanding this section of the defence. Colonel Butler ordered Battalion to move up to the Chateau at eastern end of Point 63 as there had been practically no firing. Major Prowse did not place much reliance on the Dorset report and sent his Adjutant to Colonel Butler to report the situation, as he believed it to be. Colonel Butler ordered that the Battalion was to be ready to support the Dorsets and that a senior officer was to go to Point 63 to take charge of the situation. Major Prowse accordingly went up there himself with 'H' Company. 'C' Company started on to it's original position to support the French attack. At 8.40 p.m. a message came from Lieutenant Ford's patrol that the French attack was not going to be pressed home and 'C' Company was accordingly recalled. Shortly afterwards the report that the Germans having broken the line was found not to be true and all companies returned to bivouac from Point 63. Whole Battalion was digging 2nd line trenches in two reliefs this morning from 7.00 a.m. to 11.00 a.m.

> It was very quiet early in the morning owing to mist. We dug trenches from 7.00 to 9.00 a.m. At about 10.00 a.m. the mist cleared and the Germans began to shell the wood in which we were lying. This continued all day with no loss except from their last shell which fell in one of our dug-outs, killing one man blowing both his arms off, and a piece blew off one man's leg between the foot and the knee.
> (*G. Prideaux*)

6th November

Quiet day. Lieutenant Ford kept in touch with the French during day, but they did not attack. Battalion relieved the Lancs Fusiliers in the trenches north of St Yves tonight. The night was foggy so the moon did not interfere with the relief, which was a difficult one owing to the German trenches being within 100 yards of ours. Very cold night – 47 reinforcements arrived tonight.

7th November

Enemy made heavy attack by two battalions against line St Yves-Le Gheer. Artillery bombardment of the trenches (held by Worcesters) started about 5.00 a.m. At about 7.30 a.m., a large number of Germans broke through the centre of the Worcester line, after the Worcesters had been driven out of their trenches by shellfire. There was a thick fog until about 8.30 a.m, which enabled the Germans to advance undetected. The Irish Fusiliers first reported the penetration of the line to Major Prowse about 10.00 a.m. Information was asked of the O.C. of the Worcesters as to the actual situation and a reply was received that it was all right. The trenches and houses which had been occupied were not however recaptured, though attempts were made by the Inniskilling Fusiliers and East Lancs. Both attempts being repelled with great loss to us. Two platoons Lancs Fusiliers were sent up to secure the right flank of the Irish Fusiliers. East Lancs held Le Gheer and Inniskillings the eastern edge of wood. Our companies had been disposed 'A' on right – 'C' in centre – 'B' on left and 'H' in reserve. Tonight 'H' relieved 'A' on the right trenches which been heavily shelled. 'A' lost 3 killed and 5 wounded.

Heavy bombardment on our right followed by sharp rifle-fire. It was first reported that the Germans had broken through and they certainly were doing a lot of shouting. A later report said they were driven back and retiring across our front, it was too foggy to see them and help them on their way. Heavy shelling all day and Jerry has now got some first class snipers. We dare not show above the parapet of the trench. My chum, Private F. Hyde foolishly poked his head over the top and a second later was lying at the bottom of the trench with a bullet through his head. The trenches in places are very shallow. Relieved in the evening by 'H' Company and went back to reserve at Headquarters in the sunken road. We had to dig our own trench, so I and three men dug one five feet deep, curled up in it and had a lovely sleep.
(*Arthur Cook*)

Stand to Arms at 5.00 a.m. Dig again, snipers in rear as well as in front. Jack Cove shot, rather a trying day; relieved at 8.00 p.m. and went in reserve; put in charge of a guard.
(*Edward Packe*)

A trench was blown in by a big shell and seven men were buried alive. Sergeant F Harris left his own trench under heavy rifle and shellfire got out four men and re-dug the trench which covered an important approach. This was done in broad daylight with the enemy within 150 yards.
(*Lt Col C B Prowse*)

8th November

Not much shelling today. 'H' Company had no casualties in forward trench. The Germans are definitely located in the trench which used to be occupied by 'H' Company and Machine Gun Section. Also in buildings on eastern edge of Ploegsteert Wood, including two which were used on 26th October as Battalion Headquarters and dressing Station respectively. No effort was made today to turn the Germans out of their position but the Inniskilling Fusiliers were ordered to block the wood. Captain Maud and 47 N.C.O.s and men from England arrived today – posted 'B' Company.

I was told later about the capture of the German prisoner by 'C' Company. He was found by their listening patrol wandering about near 'C' Company lines at night, having lost his way. They fired on him and he dropped on the ground and lay as if he was dead. The Commander of 'C' Company was sent for, and when he saw the man he told the patrol to bury him. One of the men joking-

ly put the muzzle of his rifle against the man's head, when to everybody's great astonishment the man jumped up, saying, "Nein! Nein!"
(*G. Prideaux*)

9th November

'H' Company heavily shelled in forward trench today. An attempt was made tonight to drive Germans out of their position east of Ploegsteert Wood. This was made by East Lancs and Argyll and Sutherland Highlanders. Owing to faulty timing it was a failure. The Germans split the attack in two and inflicted great loss on our troops. An officer and 50 of Royal Scots Fusiliers were sent up to guard exits from northeast corner of Ploegsteert Wood and were disposed along southern edge of St Yves village.

> During the night, unperceived and unheard by us, three companies of French infantry advanced along our left flank and dug themselves in facing us at about 300 yards range. Early in the morning our lookouts noticed a new trench facing us with men in blue hats walking about in it. They immediately opened fire, when a man in the trench jumped on the parapet and waved his arms excitedly. Soon, however, we saw he was a Frenchman. We stopped firing, and a French sergeant strolled across to talk to us. We apologized, but he did not

Figure 9
Building Paths. (*Somerset Light Infantry Archive*)

Figure 7
St. Yves. (*Somerset Light Infantry Archive*)

seem to mind a bit, only saying that we did make them bob a bit. He told us
that they were part of the French force attacking Messines and had lost their
way, so they had dug themselves in where they were. It was very lucky that we
did not hear or see them last night, as we should have fired at them and then
they would have taken us for Germans and attacked us.
(*G. Prideaux*)

10th November

'B' Company lost heavily in right trench today, losing four killed and six wounded including Sergeant Willcox who was 'Mentioned in Dispatches'. It was not
however thought advisable to relieve them tonight as a German attack was
expected, they having brought up a Bavarian Division to Warrenton. 100 men of
the Royal Scots Fusiliers (all that was left of this Regiment.) were sent up to support us. They were disposed in trenches, which they dug that day running the
north of St Yves (behind our right trench). A very dark night. 200 of the Bedford
Regiment came up to dig a second line of trenches, but it was too dark for them
to start work until about 11.00 p.m. The Messines road below the Chateau was
heavily shelled tonight about 7.00 p.m, when supplies were being issued and
wounded evacuated, two stretcher-bearers were killed. The rest of the night was

particularly quiet; thought the Germans burnt a great many flares and seemed to expect us to attack.

11th November

Situation normal – much rain and cold. Scots Fusiliers relieved Argyll and Sutherland Highlanders tonight.

> Relieved 'B' Company after dark in advanced trenches. Wet night and very cold. Trenches are full of water, nowhere to sit down, or lie down, only to stand up with water over your boots in inky blackness. Occasionally a shell smothers you with mud and earth. What an existence for human beings.
> (*Arthur Cook*)

12th November

Argyll and Sutherlands relieved by Worcesters this morning. Quiet day. Gunners destroyed an estaminet today, facing 'C' which Germans had been seen using the previous night.

> Came back from the Listening Post at dawn, helped to dig a "Jack Johnson" proof trench. Knocked off and tried to go to sleep in the new J.J. proof trench but one of our 4.5" howitzers dropped a shell on the parapet over my head and buried me from the waist down. Shelled intermittently during the day. Relieved at dark and moved into the flank trench again, facing Messines.
> (*Edward Packe*)

13th November

Rained hard all day. Very little shelling or sniping near us. Rifle Brigade relieved the Battalion tonight. We moved into trenches in Ploegsteert Wood. The rides in the wood were almost 3 feet deep in mud and movement was difficult. Result was that relief was not completed until 5.30 a.m.on 14th.

> In the morning a gunner officer came up to my trench in order to observe the fire of a howitzer battery which had been ordered to demolish a house about 100 yards to our right front. The battery made the most wonderful shooting. They first fired a round of shrapnel with the gun laid by the map, i.e., range measured from a map, and directed by bearing in order to see whereabouts the shot would go. The shell burst about 75 yards over and about 10 minutes right. He corrected the battery by telephone, and then they fired a lyddite shell, which was nearer still. They hit the house with their 3rd, 5th, 8th and 10th

From:	**11th Brigade**
To:	**Rifle Brigade, Hampshires, East Lancs, Somerset L.I**
Time:	**1129**

It is intended to continue shelling of the enemy's trenches, east of Ploegsteert Wood. There is some danger from splinters of the heavy howitzers shells to men in our own trenches, but this can be entirely avoided if our men lie low in their trenches when they hear the shell coming and remain lying low for 30 seconds or more after the shell has burst. They should not bob up to see the result of each shell.

shots and blew it to pieces. Two Germans ran out of the house after it had been hit. I had some men with rifles waiting for them, but they missed them, unfortunately.
(*G. Prideaux*)

Slept in a splendid 'booby-hutch' and enjoyed ourselves there till the Germans blew the side in. The Germans started shelling and I spent most of the afternoon in our dugout, went out into the trench for a few minutes as one of the men in the trench was getting windy, when we got back to the dugout we found one shell had blown the end of the dugout in. It came on to rain in a bloody manner and we got soaking wet. Eventually relieved by the Rifle Brigade and we got back into rotten bad trenches in the wood, a shivering cold night. (*Edward Packe*)

14th November

Battalion Headquarters built by Engineers in middle of wood. Battalion Headquarters moved this afternoon into a house at 9th Kilostone on Ploegsteert-Messines road which is used as a Report centre for this section of the defences. 'A' Company moved into billets at a farm near Battalion Headquarters. Cold rain continued today. Supplies had to be manhandled up to the trenches through the wood. This was a very long job, even though it could be done by day. 2/Lieutenant Parr rejoined today with 60 N.C.O.s and men including some who had been sent away sick.

15th November

Rained hard all day. Very wretched for men in the trenches which are mostly half full of water. Major Prowse, Commanding the battalion, has been given Brevet Lieutenant Colonelcy for 'Gallant conduct in the field'. News was received today and was received with great pleasure by all ranks. Lieutenant Colonel Prowse was

From:	**Brigadier General Hunter Weston**
To:	**Lieutenant Colonel Prowse**
Time:	**2212**

Hurrah, Hurrah, Hurrah. My heartiest congratulations from self and staff and from all your brother officers in the 11th Infantry Brigade. No honour in this war has been more thoroughly deserved.

From:	**Brigadier General Hunter Weston**
To:	**Somerset Light Infantry**
Time:	**2215**

You will rejoice to hear that Major Prowse has been given Lieutenant Brevet Colonelcy for distinguished conduct in the field. No one more thoroughly deserves this promotion and it is an honour not only to himself but the fine Battalion he has commanded so well. My heartiest congratulations to all ranks on this honour to your C.O.

not present, he having been sent for two days to Divisional H.Q.

The first snow of the winter. Had some cocoa and bread and butter for breakfast. Shaved and washed, dried clothes and sewed on buttons at the Farm. Detailed for guard on Divisional Headquarters at Nieppe, fell in at 1.30 p.m. and arrived Nieppe at about 5.00 p.m., out of gunfire at last. Mounted the guard, then managed to get some sleep. Visiting Rounds at 11.00 p.m.
(*Edward Packe*)

I received you parcel quite safe. I was very pleased to get it as it is a change from what we have been getting. I am glad to hear that Harry has joined the army and I hope he will get on all right. Tell him that if he comes our here, not to be afraid but make a good trench for himself and then when he gets attacked by the enemy he will be all right. He will be able to let them have it while he is nearly safe himself. Tell Harry that it a grand time out here, we get plenty of thrills, I would not have missed it for all the money in the world, although I have nearly had enough now. The worst part of the war now is the cold weather in the trenches where you have not room to walk about much, but we have the satisfaction of knowing the other side are the same, but I think we are a little better off than they are because the people in England send us out such a nice lot of warm clothes. Our trenches in some place are not more than 75 yards away from the Germans and we can hear them talking and singing. They have even got a gramophone which they pinched out of the houses when they were retiring. Thing are rather quieter now than when we came out. I should think that, by the papers, that there is hardly a man in Taunton who is not a soldier. I think that it is quite right that every man who is able should do something to defend his Country. I am sure we want all we can get. I did think first along that the war would be over by Christmas but I don't think so now, I will give it until about the middle of 1915. Well I think that is all for now.

(Bert Hooper, Somerset County Gazette)

Chapter Nine

'Plug Street'
16th November–11th December

16th November

Still very wet though not so much rain as the last few days. Battalion moved into frontline trenches on the eastern edge of Ploegsteert Wood to relieve the Lancs Fusiliers. East Lancs are on our right and Rifle Brigade on our left. Headquarters moved up from the house at 9th Kilostone on Ploegsteert-Messines road to R.E. hut. Captain Allfrey went home today as A.D.C. to General Snow, Commander, 27th Division.

17th November

C.O. went round the trenches this morning. It had rained all night so that the trenches were soaking wet and men had slept very little. Supplies were manhandled last night by 'B' Company from the house at 9th Kilostone to our Headquarters through heavy mud. This work occupied about twelve hours and was a great strain on the men. The supply issuing point was accordingly changed to the farm 400 yards south in Ploegsteert Wood and a track cut through the wood to it. This was found to be a great improvement and the supplies of the Battalion could be got up by about 30 men in about 1 1/2 hours in the dark. Colonel Prowse returned from Nieppe today. The house at 9th Kilostone was heavily shelled today and evacuated. A fine day.

> Sergeant Major Church reported that there were some bodies we could bury where our trench went back at right angles in the wood, so I decided to do so. I found men of all different regiments lying out there and it was impossible to identify them as the Germans had taken their identity discs away and had rifled their pockets. We buried most of them and whilst this was going on I went for-

117

ward to the edge of the wood to have a look at the German trenches. I found a sniper's post with plenty of ammunition and the trench which we thought occupied by the Germans unoccupied except for some dead bodies. I made a rough sketch of the German lines and detected no movement and so was just returning to our own lines when Church came up and wanted to have a look. The Germans unfortunately spotted us then, but we ran back into the wood and were under cover before they fired. We were both hit, but not the men who were acting as burial party. I went back and got Church carried in safely. His leg had been broken. We then both had our wounds dressed and I walked back to Battalion Headquarters where they gave me an excellent breakfast.
(*W Whittuck*)

To start off with, I was lucky enough to be picked to go on General Divisional Headquarters Guard, so here we are, thirty of us about five miles behind the firing line. I am corporal of the guard every other day and you would laugh to see me shouting 'Old Guard....present Arms.'
(*Edward Packe*)

18th November

Captain Campbell O.C. 'A' Company was wounded today and the command of his company was taken over by Lieutenant Whittuck. Fine bright day. Hard frost tonight. Very much more comfortable than the mud.

Rise and have a wash, take over guard for Sergeant Webber, have a pretty slack day. Several prisoners and stragglers brought in. Sleep on a feather bed. Visiting Rounds at 11.30 p.m. Meaden caught sleeping on duty. I have just been writing a couple of letters for a chap who can't write.

There are several classes of guns. Little ones that must be quite close and give you no warning when they are coming and bigger guns whose shells you can hear coming. One 'Johnson' about a week ago buried a whole section with one shell, they only dug four out alive and they were off their heads with the shock (probably a latrine rumour, I didn't see this happen).
(*Edward Packe*)

From:	**Somerset Light Infantry, Rifle Brigade, Hants, E Lancs**
To:	**11th Brigade**
Date:	**18th November 1914**

The Major General commanding wishes it to be clearly understood throughout his Brigade that the business of officers and NCOs is to direct the action of their unit or sub-unit and that it is wrong for a commander to relinquish this, his proper duty, in order to attend to a wounded man.

Figure 11
Hunter Avenue. (*Somerset Light Infantry Archive*)

19th November

Very cold indeed today, snow and frost. Lieutenant Whittuck was badly wounded today. Lieutenant Prideaux took over command of 'A' Company on his return from guard duty at Divisional H.Q. at Nieppe. Quiet day.

> Come off guard at 9.30 a.m., have a wash. Go out and get lunch. Get kit ready to move. March out at 4.30 p.m. and it snows like mad. Arrive in trenches in Ploegsteert Wood. Spend a rotten night in a tiny hole with Tim Holley and manage to get a little sleep, much to Tim's amazement.
> (*Edward Packe*)

20th November

Still very cold and frosty. More comfortable than damp weather. Rifle Brigade relieved Lancs Fusiliers in reserve trenches. R.E. started building new Headquarters for the Battalion about 300 yards north of present hut.

In the evening a platoon of the London Rifle Brigade with two officers

Figure 12
Dugouts. (*Somerset Light Infantry Archive*)

Captains Hussey and Morrison, relieved some of our men in order to learn something of trench life. I put them between our own men and put them on sentry-go together. One of the L.R.B.s was hit before we got to the trench. He made no sound, so in the darkness he was never noticed until the next morning, when, we found him where he had been hit. It froze hard.
(*G Prideaux*)

Our trenches take a very curious angle here. Just on our left is a hedge running straight from the wood to the German line for about 100 yards and by the side of it is a trench which bears sharply left, forming a letter Z. This I think is dangerous. It is a splendid landmark and open to enfilade fire.

We are within 200 yards of the enemy. I had a narrow escape today. The Germans are using a very quick firing gun known as a 'Whizz-bang.' I was sitting in the trench with my back to the enemy and my waterproof sheet stretched across the trench to keep the rain off. One of these shells came through the parapet a foot above my head, tore my ground sheet and burst on the back of the trench. I was covered with mud and a lot went down the back of my neck.

I was not feeling too well in the afternoon so went along to the sick bay where I had a fairly easy night.
(*Arthur Cook*)

21st November

Still very cold, had frost again. Line readjusted today. Rifle Brigade took over our right Company trench. 'H' Company moved into billets at Farm on Ploegsteert-Messines road in reserve. Battalion is now holding a line set at eastern edge of wood. Two companies in firing line, one in support trenches, one in reserve. Rifle Brigade H.Q. were to have moved into our hut today and we to new hut, but latter not being ready, move postponed until tomorrow. 2nd Lieutenant Edwards and 59 other ranks joined Battalion from England.

22nd November

'H' Company went to Pont De Nieppe to wash under divisional arrangements. The scheme is that they move to billets in Pont De Nieppe overnight, wash next day and are provided with clean clothing. After washing they are moved to clean set of billets at Armentieres and return to the supporting trenches on the third day. This arrangement has been made possible by the London Rifle Brigade coming up and relieving the reserve companies in their billets in Ploegsteert. On the 20th 4 platoons of London Rifle Brigade were put with our men in the trenches, an equivalent number of our men being sent back to London Rifle Brigade at Romarin. This gives about 170 of our men a rest in addition to the company washing at Nieppe. The London Rifle Brigade men are mixed up with our men and not separate as a platoon at present. 'B' Company relieved 'C' in left trench tonight. This relief was made difficult by the snow lying on the ground, but was carried out without casualties. Battalion Headquarters moved to new hut 300 yards north of the old one which was taken over by Rifle Brigade. Very cold night, hard frost.

23rd November

Very cold day. Spent most of day settling down in new Battalion Headquarters and making it bullet proof. Quiet day.

24th November

Lieutenant Moore and 56 other ranks arrived from England last night. (They stopped in a farm with stretcher-bearers last night and joined their companies this morning.) Frost began to break this afternoon and clouds rolled up. It had been arranged for supplies to be brought up 24 hours ahead, so that we could get following days supplies to Headquarters by daylight and companies could draw them from there as soon as it is dark.

During the day I put up any amount of barbed wire along our right flank,

which was drawn back into the wood, as that bit of the wood is held by the Germans, who had broken through the Worcesters' lines on November 7th. Whilst on this job I found any number of dead bodies (English) lying in the wood about 80 yards from our trench. They are mostly Inniskillings, who had tried to turn the Germans out of the wood. It is impossible to bury them, as we are only 70 yards from the German trenches. In the evening the enemy opened fire again but we took no notice. Still freezing.
(*G Prideaux*)

At 7.30 a.m. the company marched to a large linen factory, which had been rigged up as a washing place. The men marched into a big warehouse, where they took off their service dress (coats and trousers), tied them together with their identity disc and put them on a red barrow, which was then taken to the fumigator. They then were marched into the bleaching room, where there were 15 large vats of hot water ready. Here they took off all their clothes – which were boiled in disinfectant – were supplied with soap and towel and had a thoroughly good wash, ten men a vat with as much hot water as they wanted. After they have dried themselves they are supplied with fresh underclothing, shirt, socks, pants, and a vest. When they have put on these they go into the warehouse again. Then the service dress is brought in on white barrows, having been disinfected and ironed. A large number of women are employed, who iron the service dress and the disinfected underclothing (if it is worth it) and mend it ready to be issued out to somebody else. The whole company of about 170 men were washed in about an hour and a quarter."
(*Lieutenant G. R. Parr*)

25th November

Milder night, with some rain. Mud everywhere again, though not a regular thaw as yet. R.E. working parties formed as usual for work on breastworks. Gangways were made today from Battalion Headquarters to left of right company trench to conduct supporting parties up to trench. Everything very quiet today. Distinct thaw today, though weather cold and raw. Lieutenant Moore took over temporary command of 'H' Company. Lieutenant Bradshaw who had been wounded on November 2nd returned today, took over command of 'A' Company.

The thaw started today and everything was soon ankle deep in mud. It rained hard, and when I woke up I found that I was lying in a pool of water. Today we were told that we were going to be relieved on the 27th, when we shall have been in the front trench for 11 days without a break. In the morning we had one man wounded in the hand by a shrapnel shell. In the afternoon, whilst we were winding barbed wire off a reel, Sergeant Dagger had a bullet through his head and some splinters struck Sergeant Munday and another private in the head. It certainly looks as if they are firing explosive bullets.
(*G Prideaux*)

Figure 13
Machine gunners. (*Somerset Light Infantry Archive*)

We have had two lots of snow and the water in our water bottles has been solid ice and several people have had to go sick with frostbite, but it has now thawed out again and the trenches are filthy muddy again. We are entrenched just inside a wood on the outskirts of a village and so far have no lyddite shells at us for which we are more than thankful. I share a 'house' with another chap which we built between us, it is about 8 feet long and 7 feet deep roofed over with boughs, then straw, then earth and will keep out shrapnel bullets, but as a friend of mine remarked the other day 'Old Jack ain't particular where he comes in.' Yesterday I went out with chaps to put up barbed wire on a flank in the wood in case they try to attack us that way and By Jove, when we had finished (I was doing the outside lot, there were three of them) I had a job to find my way in and it was broad daylight, so if they try and rush us by night heaven help them.

Please excuse bad writing. Our artillery is shelling one or two houses close to this wood in which the Germans have had a Maxim and have worried us a bit with sniping and although the shells are bursting about 150 yards away they literally shake the ground. (Here's another xxxxxx-----) the devil was short and none too far from this trench, please note the tail on the 'O' in 'another' was written above and witness if I lie when I say they shake.

The snipers are never quiet, day or night, and must waste an awful lot of ammunition. There total bag is three, two sergeants and a private; I'm afraid

Figure 14
Trenches, Ploegstreet. (*Somerset Light Infantry Archive*)

one of the sergeants won't live but the other two ought to be all right. The artillery are putting their 6" over us very nicely now and I think they are finding their target as a lump of brick as big as a plum has just dropped outside our trench. You can only just hear the gun fire, then you hear a noise starting very feint, like the wind in the trees, but increasing in volume and going up the scale till it sounds like an express train going through a station, then a bump and then a hell of a row and after a bit, pieces of shell and brick start dropping all around.
(*Edward Packe*)

26th November

Thaw continued today and everywhere is very muddy. Raw foggy day, very quiet. 4th Division siege howitzers shelled houses today for about two hours as our left trench reported them full of Germans. Their shells fell short into our trenches and we asked them to cease firing.

Our artillery shell a house about 80 yards from our trenches, bricks and oddments fly all over the place, some dropping pretty close. Frank Bradshaw

returns and takes over our Company again. Not a bad day.
(*Edward Packe*)

27th November

Fine warm sunny morning, turning showery later. Very quiet day. Practically no
shelling in our section. Much sniping tonight, probably due to bright moon.

28th November

Dull morning, brightened up considerably later. Our interpreter rejoined yesterday, as there was no accommodation in our hut we sent him back to live with the
Quartermaster at Rabot, where he will be more usefully employed. Strong southwest gale got up in the evening, complete thaw and much warmer. Wood keeps
paths pretty dry at present. Germans shelled between 10.00 p.m. and 3.00 a.m,
putting about 50 shells near our supply issuing farm, no damage done. A great
deal of sniping during the night.

29th November

Very dull day, no actual rain. Paths began to get muddy again. Quiet day, more
shelling at night near our supply farm, also some sniping. There is much more
sniping at night than by day.

Had a lovely hot bath and change of clothing this morning. On arrival at the
Brewery we undressed in a room taking off everything except shirt and boots.
Our khaki coat, trousers and cap, less the chinstrap, were tied in a bundle and
placed in a fumigator and vest, pants and socks were carted off, lice and all, for
boiling. We then had to go out into the open along the towpath for about 50
yards, in full view of the ladies on the bank. We had only a shirt on and it was
windy and bitterly cold so we did not loiter for their benefit. The high wind
did not help our modesty. The bathtubs were large beer vats and ten men were
allotted to each vat. We were soon in like a lot of excited kids. Every now and
then we had a peep over the side to see if our boots were O.K., as we were told
they were likely to be pinched. We were now a very lousy crowd for the lack
of washing had bred lice by the thousand and the surface of our bath water was
soon a thick scum of these vermin. We scratched each other's backs to ease
the itching. Towels and soap were ready and when we were dry we got a clean
shirt. Then we had to go back along the canal bank where the girls were still
waiting. It must have been very cold for them but I suppose they thought it
worthwhile. We got clean underclothes and our uniforms came out all steam-
ing hot. What a sight we looked with our clothes all creases and our caps all

Figure 15
Bath house, Nieppe. (*Somerset Light Infantry Archive*)

shapes! But before long the lice in the seams which had not been destroyed in
the washing came out again and we were soon scratching once more.
(*Arthur Cook*)

30th November

Cloudy day with a great deal of rain. 'H' Company went to Nieppe under the new
system which is that each battalion has a reserve company back there in billets
for three days. This means that each company is 6 days in the trenches and 3 days
in supporting trenches. Very quiet day though a great deal of sniping at night.

> In portions of the line the enemy's trenches were only 150 yards away and his
> snipers, with telescopic sights fixed to their rifles, waited and watched day and
> night for a chance shot at officers and men who unwarily exposed their heads or
> any part of their bodies above the parapets of the trenches. The utmost caution
> was necessary when moving about, a minute's forgetfulness to "keep down" and
> there was a sharp crack, followed generally by the thud of a falling body. Trees,
> bushes, the tumbled ruins of houses and cottages, all provided cover for snipers.
> (*Adapted from History*)

Figure 16
Soilders Bathing. (*Contemporary News*)

Allowed out after getting pay, so go and have a good lunch. Fall-in at 2.30 p.m. and march up to reserve trenches in Ploegsteert Wood, not a bad night. (*Edward Packe*)

1st December

Reinforcements of Lieutenant Hudson and 50 men reported this morning. 2nd Lieutenant. Braithwaite rejoined from hospital. 'C' Company trench was flooded in one part today by a spring of water. It was decided to dam this part of the trench up and evacuate and build a breastwork, as any attempt to dig drains only brings more water in. Very muddy everywhere today. Not much actual rain, very blustery.

2nd December

Rather heavy shelling today. No damage done. Dull day but not much actual rain a few showers. Moonlight night and quite warm. HM King George V inspected 'H' Company at NIEPPE today.

From:	**Somerset Light Infantry, Rifle Brigade, Hants, E Lancs**
To:	**11th Brigade**
Date:	**2nd December**

Following message receive from O.C. left trench begins 'Firing on German trench has stopped. The shellfire from guns yesterday evening demolished most of it.' Please inform guns and tell them their shelling yesterday evening had a very quietening effect on snipers.

From:	Somerset Light Infantry
To:	11th Brigade
Date:	2nd December

More shelling today. Average about two heavy howitzer and four 10lb shrapnel per hour from WARNETON and DEULEMONT directions respectively. No blind shells reported. Work done on left trench, 20 yards communications trench dug. Latrines and drainage improved. Right trench being reconstructed owing to wet. No hostile movements noticed

3rd December

Colder today and strong SW wind. Heavy rainstorms with bright intervals. 'B' Company platoon started work on some new dugouts near Battalion Headquarters in morning and in afternoon worked at cutting brushwood for the floor of the left trench which is in a very wet state. 'H' Company reports the billet in Nieppe is a good one with good washing arrangements for officers and men. Lieutenant Prideaux to hospital today with broken ankle result of an accident.

> Have to go to Divisional Headquarters for a Summary of Evidence to be taken for a Court Martial. Work on breastwork on return. Start on new 'house' and work far into the night. Frequent showers.
> (*Edward Packe*)

From:	Somerset Light Infantry
To:	11th Brigade
Date:	3rd December

Would you please always give notice when our guns are going to shell houses in L7A. No notice was received today and a blowback from first shells has dangerously wounded a man in right trench.

From:	4th Division
To:	11th Brigade, repeated to S.L. I.R.B, Hants, E Lancs
Date:	3rd December

When troops are marching with slung arms they will not be required to slope or trail arms when called to attention for the purpose of paying a compliment. Officers will call their commands to attention, give the command 'EYES RIGHT' or 'EYES LEFT' and themselves salute with the hand.

From:	Somerset Light Infantry
To:	11th Brigade
Date:	3rd December

Shelling rather heavy today. About 6 an hour from WARNETON direction. No blind shells. Both trenches improved with sandbag breastworks and timber revetments. A house in front of left trench which was much used by German snipers and which we have tried to burn down was totally destroyed today by a German shell.

4th December

Very cold wind from southeast. A force pump was set up for the right trench, part of which is waist deep in water. Not very much rain today.

5th December

Rained hard practically all day. The tracks in the wood are now in a very bad state the mud being knee deep almost everywhere. This makes it very hard for parties carrying rations etc to get along. Field General Court Martial today at Romarin today on Corporal Kilman, Privates Meaden and Lawrence. Rain stopped in evening and it was a fine bright moonlight night. O.C. 'A' Company reported during the night that owing to the risk of water the position in his trench was critical and he wanted sandbags at once for making a breastwork. These were asked for at 12.30 a.m and obtained at 6.30 a.m.

> A miserable day of rain. Have to go into Romarin to give evidence for a Court Martial; buy some food on the way back to Ploegsteert. Go and fetch some wood for the 'floor'. Very cold during the night.
> (*Edward Packe*)

From:	4th Division
To:	11th Brigade, repeated to S.L. I.R.B, Hants, E Lancs
Date:	4th December

Following message received from II Corps.

A suspicious character, description follows, has been reported to have been asking questions at the day H.Q of Divisional R.A. and 15th F.A.B. whilst only civilian inhabitants were there.

Description – Big man strongly built, dark hair and small moustache. Scar on left of nose. He was dressed in khaki but had no equipment or badges of rank. Talked English but not like other English soldiers.

This man, if seen, should be sent under escort to Divisional H.Q.

From:	4th Division
To:	11th Brigade, repeated to S.L. I.R.B, Hants, E Lancs
Date:	4th December

German soldier in uniform with spiked helmet visited REBEQUES FARM, near LE BIZET at 6.45 a.m. this morning. He was riding a bicycle and he spoke to the woman who owns the farm and asked if my officers were there and threatened to shoot her with his revolver.

Report if any unit missed a bicycle last night or today.

6th December

Some sandbags carried by London Rifle Brigade, others brought up by our transport wagons. Towards morning there was quite a sharp frost and it was very cold. The frost did not harden the paths at all. Quite a fine morning – bright sun. Got cloudy in the afternoon and by 5.00 p.m. was raining hard again. Sent an urgent message this evening for a force pump for our right trench, which is knee deep in water, though the dugouts are fairly dry. This pump came during the night and was carried up with great labour – very dark night. Company Quartermaster Sergeant Ricketts was killed after taking out rations to 'H' Company in left trench.

7th December

Trenches in very bad state after last night's rain. Continual pumping and bailing does not suffice to keep the water down. The right platoon in the left trench ('H' Company) were withdrawn today into Ploegsteert Wood, as their trench is knee deep in water. It will only be occupied at night in future. The gap caused by this trench being filled in with barbed wire and a barricade of sandbags is being cre- · ated across the road at northeast corner of wood. It rained hard all day today driving in heavily from the SW. Wind rose to a gale in the evening. Very wet night and very dark.

> In 1914 trench warfare was still in its infancy. The trenches, often dug of necessity in soft ground, were vastly different from the scientific constructions in which men lived and fought in later periods. Some of them were mere excavations in the ground, the earth thrown up to form the parapet, behind which men crouched and watched the enemy. Sandbags were scarce and men were often shot through the parapet, the bullet first penetrating the soft earth.
>
> There were no trench-boards to walk upon, and dugouts were primitive in construction. In front of the trenches the barbed-wire entanglements were of a simple character.

Figure 17
Flooded Trenches. (*Contemporary Magazine*)

Since the 25th October, on which date the Battalion Diary recorded that the trenches were "absolute quagmires," conditions had grown steadily worse. On that date the water and mud were ankle-deep in the front lines; by the beginning of November the trenches, in places, were knee-deep in slime and filth. The stench from dead bodies, often partially buried in the spongy, slimy ground, just as they had fallen, was awful. Unwashed, caked with mud, clothes sodden, the British soldier, aching with rheumatism and the early symptoms of trench feet, verminous and generally in a deplorable condition, held the line.

The Lys River ran through country practically sea level, therefore very low-lying. Numerous small tributaries branched in all directions from the main waterway, intersecting the country, and in many places forming boggy or marshy ground which in wintertime became waterlogged. Quite half of the Bois de Ploegsteert (the southern half) was on sea level, but the northern portion was on slightly higher ground, rising gradually to Point 63. The line held by the Battalion, however, about St. Yves, lay between two small tributaries of the Lys, the Warnave on the south and the Douve on the north. When the winter rains began the countryside generally became sodden and the digging of trenches and dugouts, without the necessary means of draining them, became an almost hopeless task. Moreover, the ground in the neighbourhood of the trenches was pock-marked with gaping shell holes, into which water trickled, forming nauseous pools in which the mangled remains of friend and foe lay rotting, poisoning the air with sickening odours.

THE BRITISH UNDER FIRE—AND ALMOST UNDER WATER.
During the incessant rain in Flanders the lot of our men in the trenches was such   gave comparatively little warmth. Where this could be done,
that they had to be relieved as quickly as possible.   Rubber boots and leggings   structures were used for protection, and the ground was covered
were but slight palliatives, and coke braziers, while they cast a ruddy glow around,   and straw. Sometimes it was possible to pump out the water.

Figure 18
Pumping out the trenches. (*Contemporary Magazine*)

The terrible condition of the battlefield made attacks by both sides, at all times, difficult. "The deadly accuracy, range and quick-firing capabilities of the modern rifle and machine gun require that a fire-swept zone be crossed in the shortest possible space of time by attacking troops. But if men are detained under the enemy's fire by the difficulty of emerging from a water-logged trench, and by the necessity of passing over ground knee-deep in holding mud and slush; such attacks become practically prohibitive owing to the losses they entail."

For hours on end men had to stand in trenches, often three feet deep in water, with a gale of wind blowing and in a driving rain, wet to the skin, shivering and shaking from cold and worn with fatigue.

(*Adapted from History*)

8th December

Dull day; though not much actual rain during the day. 'H' had a very bad time as their pump had broken down and the water was rising rapidly. The London Rifle Brigade Company came in about 5.00 p.m. and the relief was completed by 8.00 p.m. They had a very bad night; much rain and water in trench rose to about 2ft deep during the night

9th December

Cold foggy day – not much rain. London Rifle Brigade reported their trench falling in and required much revetting material. Accordingly all available men were turned on to cut timber, collect sand bags and wire, and this was sent to the Moated Farm in the evening and taken out after dark. An R.E. party came up to assist in revetting the trench but reported they could do nothing until water was cleared out, which would have required about six pumps. No pumps are available.

10th December

Application made to 11th Brigade for pumps for trenches. None are forthcoming at present. C.O. decided to relieve London Rifle Brigade Company after 48 hours in the left trench, as conditions there are so bad. 'B' Company accordingly moved into the left trench tonight. The men have to stand in water the whole time they are in the trench and most of the dugouts are awash also the latrines. A small party of R.E. under Lieutenant Wright went into the trench tonight and worked hard at the revetting work. Eventually a corner of the trench was abandoned as hopeless and the communication trench was converted into a drain and water from the dugouts baled into it. All connections with it being dammed off. This had the effect of keeping the dugouts drier but cut off the only means of communications between platoons by day. By night it is possible to get from one

From:	11th Brigade
To:	S.L. I.R.B, Hants, E Lancs
Date:	10th December

Meeting of C.O.s at 11.00 a.m. tomorrow at Brigade H.Q. C.O.s will come prepared to give a considered opinion first as to the advisability of holding their present trenches in view of their flooded conditions, secondly of the method which they would propose to adopt in case an attack from our present line was ordered. General Hunter Weston having returned from leave resumes command of Brigade. Captain Boyd resumes duties as Brigade Major.

From:	Lt Col Prowse
To:	Brig. Gen Hunter Weston
Date:	10th December

I propose with your sanction to replace the Company of L.R.B. in my left trench tonight with my supporting Company, who would have relieved them tomorrow night. I will send L.R.B. into support breastwork. I think it advisable owing to the very bad time they have had for two nights. We are going to hold the left trench all right whatever happens and if need be do it by the night relief until the weather conditions alter and the water can be got under.

I can spare my adjutant for his leave quite well as I have got a good officer to replace him and am well off for officers compared with other corps.

dugout to another by moving outside the trench, but this is attained with great risk, as there is more sniping by night than by day. Further the Germans have moved snipers up into a house within 60 yards but of our trench. We asked our guns to blow it down; but they said they couldn't do it unless our trench was evacuated. This was not considered advisable. All officers who were to have gone on leave were today called to Brigade Headquarters and informed they could not go, under the strictest secrecy, no reason being given. Lieutenant Colonel Prowse who has been suffering from neuralgia went sick today. Major E Elgar took over command.

11th December

Rained very hard today and during the night – 'B' Company had a very bad time today in the left trench. The dugouts occupied by 'H' have been flooded and these men are occupied by building themselves huts above ground. Everybody occupied today in trying to keep trenches, etc. from flooding.

From:	11th Brigade
To:	S.L. I.R.B, Hants, E Lancs
Date:	11th December

Somersets will detail 1 N.C.O and remaining battalions 1 man to report to Brigade H.Q. at 10.00 a.m. tomorrow for transfer to TRAIN in connection with distribution of Christmas gifts. These men will remain with TRAIN until further notice.

From:	Somerset Light Infantry
To:	11th Brigade
Date:	11th December

No shelling today. Wire put down in front of breastwork. Left trench revetted last night. Barbed wire in rear of right trench continued. Enemy snipers and machine guns more active. Enemy have erected poles in front of trenches probably supporting nets against hand grenades.

Chapter Ten

Attack on 'The Birdcage' 12th–23rd December

12th December

Drier today. Little actual rain although very cloudy. A new system of reliefs started today, front trenches only held with two platoons, the remaining platoons of those companies being in support. The platoons to change over daily so that the men will only have one day in the wet trench. Other two companies kept back at billets one at Stretcher-bearer Farm and one at farm west of Report Centre. At the CO's conference today the GOC informed Companies that a general advance of the Allies was contemplated that the Battalion and the Hants are to prepare to carry out an attack against the enemy who have penetrated the line east of Ploegsteert Wood about square L7a. Preparations are to be made in the day for making wire mattresses of rabbit wire and straw to get over the German wire, also our own wire is to be cut. 'A' Company reconnoitered ground in front of their trenches. The German trenches were found to be weakly held, but the ground over which the attack was to take place was broken and almost impassable. On all sides were gaping shells holes, full of water, and thick slimy mud.

13th December

Strong southwest gale today. A good deal of sun and no rain. C.O.'s conference at Brigade Headquarters lasted three hours. Somerset Light Infantry and Rifle Brigade to prepare for attack on Birdcage after the line Wytschaete-Messines has been taken. Details of attack discussed. C.O. saw O.C.'s right and left trenches, Lieutenant Moore and Capt. Bradshaw at 8.00 p.m. Lieutenant Harris was instructed to reconnoitre enemy's wire, which was found to be about 6 feet high and 6 feet thick and of considerable strength. He also started preparing gaps in hedge along south part of the trench for storming party to pass. A great deal of rain tonight.

14th December

'B' Company made mattresses out of rabbit wire stuffed with straw for crossing the German wire. The attack on Wytschaete (north of the Battalion) started at 9.00 a.m. this morning – slight progress was made. Our guns shelled heavily during the day, but no attack was made. Little response from the Germans. 'B' Company sent out patrol to reconnoitre the German wire. They were not successful in finding anything.

15th December

Dull day, some heavy showers. Supporting platoon filled in retrenchment. Headquarters built new huts as dugouts all flooded out. Capt. Richardson, Durham L I who has been posted to Battalion, joined today – took command of 'C' Company as Capt. Watson went sick today. No progress today in attack on Wytschaete. Fine night. 'B' Company reconnoitered German Wire

On the night of December 15th a call was made for volunteers, to reconnoiter

From:	11th Brigade
To:	S.L.I, R.B., Hants, E. Lancs
Date:	15th December

There will not be a conference tomorrow.

The G.O.C. would like a report as soon as possible on the result of the trials he spoke about at the conference as to the best methods of crossing the German wire entanglements, especially the tripod variety. Also as to how many rabbit wire mattresses have been made and how many more required to be made.

Please report whether sufficient planks are available and ready, and whether they are strong enough and long enough to carry an armed man over the trenches.

Practice should be carried out tomorrow in crossing trenches on planks without noise as well as crossing entanglements.

the enemy's position. Their trenches lay at varying distances – from fifty to two hundred yards – and Captain Maude desired to know how strongly they were defended, and the nature of the barbed wire entanglements. Sergeant Burge volunteered to attempt this highly dangerous and difficult task, the nature of which was not in any way minimised by the officer, who told him that he would "carry his life in his hands." Two privates pluckily offered to continue the work should Sergeant Burge be killed or so badly wounded that he could not return. It must he explained that between the British and German trenches were two farms held by the enemy, the intervening 'no mans land' being thickly strewn with shell holes and the bodies of British and Germans, many of the dead having lain there for several weeks. Divesting himself of all

[Painted specially for this work.]   [By Leslie Mosley.]

SERGEANT BURGE FEIGNING DEATH ON BEING DISCOVERED BY A DOG IN FRONT OF THE
ENEMY'S WIRE ENTANGLEMENTS.

After reconnoitring in front of the enemy's lines at Ploegsteert one night in December, 1914, Sergeant Baldwin Burge, of the Somerset
Light Infantry, had turned to go back to his trench when he heard barking. He at once lay full length on the ground, rigid as though dead,
and immediately afterwards a small dog dashed up to him from the enemy's trenches. After sniffing round him the dog, which was
accustomed to the sight of dead men, made off. The Germans, in fear of some night intrusion into their lines, were keeping up a fitful rifle-
fire and sending up flares, but fortunately Burge was not seen. For his valuable services he was rewarded with the D.C.M.

Figure 19
Sergeant Baldwin. (*Contemporary Magazine*)

his equipment, unarmed, and without a hat. Sergeant Burge, shortly after 2.00 a.m. wished his comrades goodbye, and crept through a small gap in the trench. There was no moon, but the stars were shining brightly as he slowly crawled over the scarred and deadstrewn ground. Occasionally a star shell threw a vivid light over the field, and when this happened he lay as still as the dead around him. It was a gruesome task, fraught with great danger, as all the time German snipers were on the alert. Twice he was fired at, and once a bullet hit so near that he was splashed with mud. Continuing to advance, he at length got beneath the parapet of the German trench, and could hear the enemy talking and working. He was about to move when a cough warned him of the nearness of a sentry, and it was with great caution he moved from that particular spot. Burge explained how the elevation of the rifles protruding from loop-holes was fortunately above his head, and the intermittent firing from both sides left him untouched. After covering a great deal of ground, and surveying as well as be was able the enemy's position and defences, he returned safely to the trench from which he had emerged two hours before. He had been given up for lost, and one can imagine the pleasure with which he was welcomed back. Burge reported to Captain Maude, to whom he handed a plan of the German trenches. He was complimented on the thoroughness with which he had carried out his orders, and Captain Maude promised to make special mention of his name.

(Newspaper Report) (Sergeant Burge was awarded the Distinguished Conduct Medal for this reconnaissance)

16th December

Very fine day. Much Sun. Good day for aeroplanes and many were out. 'A' Company continued filling in retrenchment. 'B' Company supporting platoon erected wire entanglement of German pattern and practiced crossing it on wire mattresses. Four men crossed 5' 6" bipod obstacle with 16 strands of wire in 65 seconds on wire mattresses. Enemy quiet.

17th December

Slight frost during night. Fine day. Aeroplanes out in morning. The filling in of retrenchment was carried on, and two platoons practiced crossing German tripod pattern barbed wire entanglement. C.O reconnoitered point of debouchment of left attacking company from southeast corner of Ploegsteert Wood. During the afternoon it became apparent from conversation with staff officers that an advance at once was not contemplated, and in the evening, names of officers recommended to go on leave were called for.

Not much rain during the day but some at night. Two chaps wounded by snipers.
(Edward Packe)

18th December

Very quiet day. A conference was held at Brigade HQ at 9.30 a.m. this morning at which orders were issued for an attack against the Germans in the Birdcage to be carried out tomorrow. Rained hard in the afternoon. C.O. called all officers together at about 4.00 p.m. and informed them of the instructions for the attack. 'B' and 'C' Companies were not to go into the trenches tonight but to remain in billets and carry out the attack tomorrow. 'A' Company held the right and left trench. 'H' Company remaining in reserve in the "Breastwork Line" in Hunter Avenue

At a conference held at 11th Brigade Headquarters definite orders were issued for the attack on the "Birdcage" to be carried out on the 19th. But the original intention of the attack – an advance – had been modified and all the 4th Division was expected to do was (to use the words of III Corps Operation Orders) "attack some point in the enemy's line, the object being to occupy the enemy on the front of the Corps and prevent him moving his reserves to meet

the French attack. The point selected for attack is the eastern end of Ploegsteert Wood between Le Gheer and St. Yves." In other words the "German Birdcage."
(*History*)

Artillery on both sides very active. One shell fell right into our trench and wounded eight men. Relieved 'H' Company in the advanced trenches on our left in the evening. A pitch-black night. I fell into several shell holes full of water and, just as I was about to get into our trench, fell into one with 3 feet of water in it. I had a job to get out as no one could see me and I was laden with a full pack, rifle and a sandbag full of food. I dared not shout for help, as we were only a few yards from the enemy lines. At last I got out after several attempts and much splashing. I felt very happy that night, I don't think! I was soaking wet up to my thighs and mud all over! I sat down in a little dugout, changed my socks, had a tot of rum and went to sleep just as I was – with plenty of lice!
(*Arthur Cook*)

One or two shells over, some rain. Relieved at 3.30 p.m. but have to come back again. Move into a different 'hut'. Eight casualties today.
(*Edward Packe*)

19th December

A clear day. About 9.00 a.m. our guns started shelling the houses and German trenches in the 'Birdcage'. At 11.00 a.m. the officer observing for the 6th Siege Battery came to Battalion Headquarters and asked for an officer to point out exactly which were our and which were the German trenches. The Adjutant was sent to the observing station at St. Yves and pointed out a trench which was about to be shelled as one occupied by the Hampshire Regiment. Several of our shrapnel shells were observed bursting over it. The attack was to be made by 'B' Company supported by 'C' Company with 'H' Company in reserve. 'B' Company lining our right trench and 'C' Company in rear of this trench. Battalion Headquarters and 'H' Company were in the breastwork line. From 1.30 p.m. until 2.30 p.m. our guns shelled very heavily but all were bursting too short. The shrapnel frequently burst over the breastwork line and the howitzers seldom pitched east of the Le Gheer-St Yves road. From 2.00 p.m. to 2.20 p.m. the Divisional machine guns and the Mountain Battery opened fire from the southern edge of the wood. The former were intended to destroy the German wire entanglement and the latter German House. The former were not successful but the latter did destroy German House. At 2.30 p.m. precisely (all watches having been set by divisional time) the attacking company dashed forward from the wood. The men carried straw mattresses, consisting of strips of wire netting stuffed with straw which were intended to throw over the wire to form a bridge. Every other man carried wire cutters. After the leading platoon on the right had advanced about

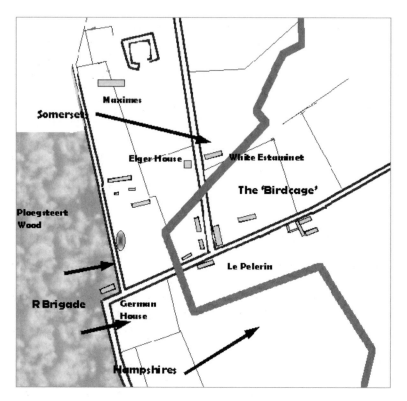

Map 9
Attack on Birdcage 19th December 1914

40 yards, a howitzer shell of ours burst amongst them and did great damage. The left platoon advanced about 50 yards but was stopped by heavy crossfire from machine guns and rifles and was held up. Lieutenant Henson being killed. The two supporting platoons of 'B' Company were not able to carry the advance much further. 'C' Company were sent in to support at about 3.15 p.m., but could get no farther than 'B' Company. Lieutenant Parr was killed while leading his platoon. Capt. Bradshaw went out from the right trench to take on Lieutenant Parr's platoon but was hit and mortally wounded. He died after an hour's suffering. At about 4.00 p.m. 'C' Company got forward to the Le Gheer-St Yves Road under cover of darkness. This position was not tenable, as it was enfiladed by houses on their right and the trench along the road was about 3ft deep in water.

The Rifle Brigade were attacking on our right did not succeed in advancing up to the road junction which was their objective. And our right joined up with their left only about 70 yards east of the wood. 'H' Company were sent on to join up with the Rifle Brigade on the right.

At about 6.00 p.m. the situation was that our left had gained about 80 yards of the road which was our objective and the line then followed about the line of the German wire until it joined the Rifle Brigade. The position, which crossed the field, was very wet and quite unsuitable for digging. However an order came from Brigade HQ to entrench the ground gained preparatory to further advance next day. The adjutant was sent back to point out the impossibility of digging on this ground and it was eventually decided to withdraw to the former trenches in the wood. It was eventually decided not to attack again next day. The only result obtained was that the enemy were driven out of the wood across which a line of breastworks was erected by the R.E. assisted by 50 London Rifle Brigade during the night and held by 1 platoon of 'H' Company. The casualties suffered by the battalion were 3 officers killed. (Captain F.S. Bradshaw, Lieutenant. G.R. Parr and Lieutenant. S.B. Henson) and 3 officers wounded and missing (Captain R.C. Orr, Captain C.C. Maud D.S.O and 2/Lieutenant K.G.G Dennys. 27 Other Ranks were killed, 52 wounded and 30 missing.

Dawn of the 19th December broke brightly. About 9.00 a.m. the guns opened fire on the houses and trenches in the German "Birdcage," but only howitzers (4.5" and 6") took part in this bombardment, as the field guns were unable to clear the Wood. The machine guns blazed away at the German wire in order to cut gaps through which the infantry might pass when the attack began. At 11.00 a.m. an officer observing for the 6th Siege Battery came to Battalion Headquarters and asked for an officer to point out exactly which were British and which were German trenches. The opposing trench systems in the early days of the War were often very close together, communications were bad and close cooperation between artillery and infantry had not attained the degree of efficiency, which existed later. The Adjutant was therefore sent off to the observing station at St. Yves, where he pointed out a trench which was just about to be shelled as one occupied by the Hampshire Regiment. Several shrapnel shells from the Divisional Artillery were even then bursting over the trenches.

By 1.00 p.m. the attacking Companies were in position: 'B' lining the right trench, i.e. the eastern edge of Ploegsteert Wood, and 'C' in rear of this trench: 'A' Company held the two trenches which formed the Battalion front: and ' H' Company, with Battalion Headquarters, in the breastwork line.

The plan of attack adopted by 'B' Company was as follows

"Two platoons commanded by 2/Lieuts. Dennys and Henson respectively, were to charge out of the wood at 2.30 p.m., pass over the German first-line trench in the 'Birdcage' and capture the second-line trench running north and south.... The remaining two platoons, commanded by 2/Lieut. Orr, were to capture the German first-line trench in the 'Birdcage' (Account by Lieutenant Dennys)"

From 1.30 p.m. to 2.30 p.m. the guns shelled the German lines, but every shell burst short. The shrapnel shells frequently burst over the breastwork line held by the Somersets, while the howitzer shells seldom pitched east of he Le Gheer-St. Yves road.

Meanwhile a mountain battery had been moved up to the eastern edge of "Plugstreet" Wood and from 2.00 to 2.30 p.m., in cooperation with the Divisional machine guns, endeavoured to tear gaps in the German wire and demolish German House. Only the latter was destroyed, the machine-gun fire (as it was eventually found) having no effect upon the hostile wire entanglements.

At 2.30 p.m. precisely, the two leading platoons of 'B' Company, closely followed by the remaining platoons, dashed forward from the edge of the wood, towards the German front line, about 120 yards away. The Somerset men climbing over the parapets of the trenches carrying, however it was easiest, their mattresses of rabbit-wire and straw, staggering through the mud and filth towards the enemy's lines; every other man carrying wire-cutters. No sooner had the platoons set foot in No Man's Land, bullets from machine guns and rifles met the advance of the Somersets.

The leading platoon had gone forward only about 40 or 50 yards, when four 4.5 shells from the Divisional Artillery fell amongst the men, inflicting considerable casualties. The survivors, however, still pressed forward and reached the house marked "A," where a small gap was found in the wire. Captain Maud, who had by now caught up the survivors of the two leading platoons, with 2/Lieut. Dennys passed through this gap, and as they did so a German ran out of the house and bolted back towards the enemy's second-line trench. This man was 15 yards from Captain Maud, who had a shot at him with his revolver. The German, thereupon, turned round and fired his rifle from the hip. Unfortunately the shot was well aimed and the bullet struck Captain Maud in the stomach, that gallant officer dying about five minutes later. Almost simultaneously 2/Lieut. Dennys was wounded in the arm and again shortly afterwards in the hip; he was afterwards taken prisoner by the enemy. Lieutenant S. B. Henson had been killed before reaching the German wire. The only other person (officer or man) who got past the German first-line trench was 2/Lieutenant R. C. Orr, and he was shot through the head and died immediately. The two supporting platoons of 'B' Company had already been absorbed into the first line when 'C' Company was sent out (at about 3.15 p.m.), but could get no farther than 'B' Company's line, which was then about half-way across No Man's Land and approximately in prolongation of the Battalion's left trench. The terrible condition of the ground, pitted with shell holes, covered with water and deep in heavy-clinging mud, made the "going" extremely difficult. Of 'C' Company, Lieut. G. R. Parr, in charge of his platoon, was well in front of his men when he was wounded in the leg by a machine-gun bullet. He fell, but immediately endeavoured to rise and carry on with the attack. He was, however, struck by another bullet and killed almost instantaneously.' Captain Bradshaw next made an attempt to go out and lead on 'B' and 'C' Companies, but he likewise was mortally wounded and died an hour later. At 4.00 p.m. 'C' Company, under cover of darkness, had reached the Le Gheer-St. Yves Road. The position was, however, untenable, as it was enfiladed by houses on the right flank and the trench along the road was 3 feet deep in water.

On the right of the Somersets the Rifle Brigade had not succeeded in advancing to the road junction, their objective, and the left of the Rifles was only about 70 yards east of the Wood. About 5.00 p.m., therefore, two platoons of 'H' Company of the Somersets which had been in support all day, were sent out to join up with the left of the Rifle Brigade. The survivors of 'B' Company were then discovered holding one room of the house "A," the Germans being in possession of an adjoining room, each side taking "pot shots" at the other through holes in the wall.

An order was received from Brigade Headquarters to entrench the ground gained preparatory to a further advance on the next day. But the Adjutant was sent back to point out the impossibility of digging in on such ground and eventually a withdrawal to the former trenches in Ploegsteert Wood was ordered. (*Adapted from History*)

We had rumours there was to be an attack today. In the morning we got orders that our artillery was going to bombard the enemy trenches from 9.00 a.m, to noon and 12.30 to 2.00 p.m. The advance is to begin at 2.30 p.m. so I expect we shall soon have fresh lodgings! 'A' Company has to give covering fire for the advance. But we are in such an awkward position it is well nigh impossible to do so, for our front line is facing 'No man's Land' over which the attack will take place and we cannot see the enemy lines on our left. It looks as though we shall be helpless spectators of this battle.

Some of our lyddite shells are falling very short. Our trenches and the German's are very close together and in one place less than 100 yards apart. Every time we snipe at them they signal a hit, or miss, with a shovel. It is a grim kind of humour! At 9.00 a.m. our heavy and light artillery started a murderous bombardment. Unfortunately for us some of the shells are falling very short and showering back earth on us, while some of the shrapnel seems to be bursting on the Warwicks on our left. At 12.30 p.m. the guns opened up again, even heavier than before. The noise was deafening, we could not hear ourselves speak. At 2.30 p.m. 'B' Company emerged from the Wood carrying large mats to scale the enemy wire entanglements. They were immediately met by a hellish fire from enemy machine guns, but carried on under terrible conditions. The ground was very broken and heavy with water and shell holes and the men could hardly walk, let alone run, handicapped with carrying the mats, so progress was very slow. To add to their difficulties our 6-inch shells were falling terribly short. I saw one fall in the middle of a dozen men killing them all. They did not want this assistance as they were getting a lot of casualties from the enemy trenches. When the survivors got to within twenty yards of their objective they found the enemy had retired to a stronger position in rear. This had masses of barbed wire in front of it. The attack halted at the enemy front trench, as it would have been madness to go on against such odds. At dusk 'C' Company went in to attack under heavy machine gun fire and got up in line with 'B' Company who were holding on between us, in 'A' Company, and the enemy, in shell holes, etc., in 'No man's Land,' as the enemy trenches they had reached were waterlogged. The attack could get no further forward and the remnants of the two companies retired under cover of darkness to the trenches in Ploegsteert Wood.

As helpless spectators of this terrible scene we were proud of our gallant comrades as they struggled over the ground in front of us, carrying those mattresses of wire and straw. It was a tragic day for the Somersets, for we had nothing in reward for the precious lives thrown away in an attempt to gain a few yards of ground not worth the life of a single Tommy. It is sad to relate that our own guns caused as many casualties as those of the enemy. Captains Maud, Bradshaw, Orr and Lieuts. Parr and Henson lost their lives and 2/Lieut. Dennys was wounded. 27 Other Ranks were killed, 52 wounded and 30 missing. It has been an awful day and I am glad it is over. The groans of the wounded were terrible, especially at night. One man was wounded as the attack started but he went on and brought back three wounded. On going out for a fourth he was killed. The night passed quietly except for a lot of Verey Lights. The enemy are expecting another attack and are not going to be caught.
(*Arthur Cook*)

You might be rather alarmed by the casualty lists owing to rather a fiasco. I had better not tell you about it now, but it was due to the telephone wire connecting us to the artillery being broken during an attack on a trench to the northeast of Ploegsteert Wood. Corporal Bonning took part in the attack, which proved abortive, the German trench being an abandoned one, and many wounded were lying on No-Man's Land. Bonning had brought in two wounded being himself wounded in the arm, and a second time in the leg; he was getting down into his own trench when a third bullet hit him in the head.
(*Edward Packe*)

There is no change in the situation.
(*Official Despatch*)

From: **Major General Sir R.H.K. Butler – 24/11/1922**

....I think the main reasons of the 'Birdcage' being a hard nut were:

1. Difficulty of observation.
2. Our fire had to stop as soon as our attack started.
3. The thick, high trees interfered with the angle of descent of shell.
4. We had an allowance of (I think) 6 rounds per gun! And two batteries of 6 guns a day – and a share in two heavy guns.
(*NA WO95 1488*)

20th December

Lieutenant. R.L. Moore was killed this morning while reconnoitering the enemy's position in front of the new breastworks built last night between German House and our right trench. A counter attack was expected today but was not delivered. The battalion is now reduced to 11 officers including the Quartermaster and Medical Officer. A quiet day. 'B' Company occupied the left trench with all the men they had left, a strength of 2 platoons. 'C' Company took over the right trench and supporting breastwork (2 platoons on each). The Rifle Brigade took over the southern face of the right trench. 'H' Company withdrew to the Piggeries Farm and 'A' Company to the Stretcher-Bearers Farm.

21st December

Major C.W Compton who had been wounded at Ligny on Aug 26 rejoined the Battalion today and took over command of the battalion. Captain Bradshaw was buried today near Somerset House. 2 platoons of 'H' Company relieved 'B' Company tonight in the left trench. A quiet day. Capt. Yatman supervised the construction of new breastworks behind the left trench tonight. This trench is getting very full of water.

From:	11th Brigade
To:	S.L.I, R.B., Hants, E. Lancs
Date:	21st December

When describing shells the following phraseology should be used. High explosive shells of less calibre than 5.9 should be termed H.E. or accurately detailed. Black Marias should be reserved for the 5.9in howitzers. Portmanteau should be applied to the 8.2in and anything above the latter calibre may be termed Jack Johnsons.

No other terms that those above will be recognised.

From:	Somerset Light Infantry
To:	11th Brigade
Date:	21st December

Captain Maud was hit in thigh whilst cutting wire. Fell in ditch and was last seen crawling towards WHITE ESTAMINET. Allowed no one to stay with him and cannot now be found, may be a prisoner. Men are sure that Captain Orr, Lieutenants Parr and Dennys were killed by rifle fire before reaching wire areas, bodies cannot be found. Lieutenant Henson's body has been found. He was killed by rifle fire whilst heading the attacking platoon. Officer in left trench reports at least 20 men killed by one of our howitzer shells. About 10 bodies can be seen; others are probably within German lines. Captain Maud was not carrying his map of Wood.

From:	11th Brigade
To:	4th Division
Date:	21st December

Our attack the day before yesterday has evidently had the desired effect, for my observation posts report greatly increased garrisons in all German trenches along our front and parties arriving in villages in rear of their lines

22nd December

Fine day. Quiet. Lieutenant Parr was buried this afternoon near Somerset House. His body had been found last night in a shell hole a short distance east of the right trench and had been brought in with difficulty under fire.

> Sent to Divisional Headquarters at Nieppe in the Morning to learn how to throw Bombs from the C.R.E. Very casual instruction, it was on Hales No.1 and No. 2 Grenades. Have a good meal and then back up to the trenches again. (*Edward Packe*)

From:	11th Brigade
To:	4th Division
Date:	22nd December

The Somerset Light Infantry has now two companies commanded by junior 2nd Lieutenants. It would be a very great advantage if some officers could be sent out from 3rd Battalion.

Chapter Eleven

The Christmas Truce
23rd–31st December

23rd December

Fine day. Colder. Orders received today for a resumption of the arrangement whereby a company goes back to NIEPPE to wash. In this case they are to be inoculated also. The London Rifle Brigade are sending a company to each Battalion to enable each one of our companies to get away. Frost at night.

24th December

Fine day. Quiet. Work commenced on new breastworks about 100 yards behind eastern boundary of wood. These are intended for the accommodation of 1st line of supports.

> I tackled the Plum Pudding on the spot, ten people had a bit but it was mostly shared by four of us and after giving some away there was about a quarter left which contained the threepenny piece. So cutting it into four we each had a piece. I had the last, which did contain one threepence so I maintained my reputation for always getting the threepence.
> (*Edward Packe*)

25th December

There was much singing in the trenches last night by both sides. Germans opposite us brought up their Regimental Band and played theirs and our National Anthems followed by 'Home Sweet Home'. A truce was mutually arranged by the men in the trenches. During the morning officers met German officers half way

Figure 20
Christmas Truce, Fraternisation. (*Contemporary Magazine*)

between the trenches and it was arranged that we should bring in our dead who were lying between the trenches. The bodies of Captain Maud, Captain Orr and Lieutenant Henson were brought in also those of 18 N.C.O.s and men. They were buried the same day. The Germans informed us that they had captured a wounded officer (this was thought to be Lieutenant K.G.G. Dennys who commanded one of the attacking platoons of 'B' Company on the 19th). There was a sharp frost last night which continued during the day and the weather was very seasonable. Not a shot or shell was fired by either side in our neighbourhood; and both sides walked about outside their trenches unconcernedly. It afforded a good opportunity for inspecting our trenches by daylight. The enemy's works were noted to be very strong. A very peaceful day.

On handing over the body of Captain Maud a Saxon officer stated he was the bravest of the brave, or words to that effect.
(*History*)

Christmas Day! Received plenty of gifts of puddings and cakes, including Princess Mary's Gift containing tobacco, cigarettes and a pipe. These I gave away but kept the case. Had a walk round Ploegsteert, for the roads are hard after the frost. The Germans made sinister use of their time here, for all the young maidens from eleven upwards appear to have been raped and are showing signs of motherhood.
(*Arthur Cook*)

A couple of Somerset bandsmen, who had left their instruments in England and were assigned to stretcher-gearing, told me a day or so after Christmas what occurred at Ploegsteert on Christmas Day. The Saxon Christmas songs of the night before had odd results. "The songs was fine," one of my informants, declared. "They sang a lot. But the best was to come. A German bloke had a cornet, and he could play it grand. He just made it talk. The songs and the tunes the cornet feller played seemed more and more like ones we knew. Some of the songs I could have sung myself. At last out came that cornet with 'Home, Sweet Home,' and nobody could keep still. We all sang, Huns, English and all." The night spent in song produced a general peacefulness of spirit all round. As day broke the Somersets saw the Saxons on top of their trenches. Soon they called out, "Come over and visit us, we are Saxons." No shots were fired. "None of our chaps started for the German trenches," continued the bandsman. "We had heard all about the white flags the Bosches had fired from under and all that. But our medical officer is a funny cove, and he got an idea in his head that started the whole thing. He said he saw a chance to give a burial to some of our dead that had been lyin' between trenches no end of a while. So he told me and my pal here to follow him, and afore we knew where he was goin', up he pops on the trench parapet. The Bosche trenches was only fifty to seventy yards in front, and up we had to get and over after that doctor. The Saxons was right there, in plain sight. I never sweat so, nor never did my pal here. We was sure there was a game on, and we would get it good as soon as we was well out of cover. Some of our dead had laid out there for eight or ten weeks, and was in a awful state. We picked up a Inniskilling officer, a captain, and got him on a stretcher – a big job – and got him back all right. No one fired a single shot. So

Figure 21
Christmas Mail. (*Contemporary Magazine*)

out that doctor sends us again. We got over near the Bosche trench and up jumps a stocky little heavyset German officer with a bushy black beard. He steps forward and says roughlike, with a scowl like he was goin' to eat us, "Get back to your trenches, we have had quite enough of you. Get back there at once." He spoke English all right, he did. We didn't need no interpreter for him. His looks went with what he said, too. We went all right. And I won't forget goin', not in this 'ere life, you can bet. That few yards seemed a sinful long way. Every step I thought "Now I'll get it, right in the back," but I didn't. We got into our trench right by our major in command, and told him what old whiskers had said and how he said it. All the major said was, "I didn't think they would really let us get our dead. I'm not surprised." But that little trip of the doctor's had fair started it. Half an hour later I could see some of our lads on our right going right over to the Bosches in the open. The major saw 'em, too. When he got 'em in his eye he said, "You can go on now, you men, and get some more of those dead in." We went. We never saw the black-bearded chap any more, either. One of the Saxon fellers who spoke pretty good English sung out and said we could go right on with what we were doin'. He said all of us could bury dead till four o'clock, and they would, too. And sure enough they did get at it pretty soon afterward. Of course with us all kicking round each other out there in the open, lots of chaps got to talkin'. The Saxons was friendly enough. One chap said to me, "You Anglo Saxons, we Saxons. We not want to fight you." I thought I'd land him one, so I said "What about the Kayser, then, old lad? What do you think of Mr. Kayser, eh?" "Bring him here, and we'll shoot him for you," said the Saxon feller, and we all laughed. But I didn't take no stock of that. I knew he was only trying to be pleasant. Some of our chaps changed cigars and cigarettes with them Huns, and had talks about all sorts of things. At four o'clock we all took cover on both sides, but there was no firing on our front that night. The next morning we kept up the callin' business. We didn't stop it for a matter of eight days. Then the Saxons was relieved by the Bavarians. The Saxons warned us agin them Bavarians. One of the Saxon blokes said to one of our sergeants, "Saxons do not like Bavarians. Shoot them like hell." There was one Saxon chap, off a bit to our left, I heard one of our lot tell about that would-n't have no truce. He was in front of the Rifle Brigade. He kept hammerin' away all through the peace, no matter what the Saxon chaps in front of us did."

An exchange of rations was a frequent occurrence during that remarkable period. Both sides agreed that tinned 'bully' had no serious rival. "Would the men who made friends with the Saxons fight them as hard afterwards?" I asked. "Sure," was the reply. "If our chaps got a chance to put the bayonet home in one of those fellers, there wouldn't be no difference in the way they would do the job. All the first moves come from them, not from us. They even said they would fire high if they got orders to fire on us. We didn't make no such foolish promise. Our lot wanted to see the German trenches bad. They wouldn't let us right in, but we saw a lot and learned a lot. We could get right up to their wire, which was no end better than ours. But it ain't now. Wait till they try goin' against our wire, and they will find we learned a thing or two."

And the little group chuckled in anticipation.
(*F Coleman, 'From Mons to Ypres with General French', 1917*)

A very curious state of affairs reigned here on Christmas Day, I don't know how it started but anyhow Germans and English were walking about in between the two trenches, hobnobbing and exchanging cigarettes etc. The Germans were not allowed near our trenches and they wouldn't allow us near theirs. There were a good many German dead near our trenches and these we brought into the middle and then they took them away to bury them and we did the same to ours. Although I wasn't up in the trenches and was lucky enough to be back in a farm for two days, I got this from one of the stretcher bearers who brought our dead in the middle and although there were many elaborations put on the story, till it got that the Germans were in our trenches and we in theirs. The bare fact is I think we each advanced into the middle and hobnobbed there. Anyhow I saw a German field service post card with a German name and address on which a chap was given. You couldn't hear a shot fired the whole day anywhere and it was awfully hard to realise that there was a war on until they came for a fatigue party from our company to bury the dead that had been brought in. Christmas Day was a beautiful cold frosty day with nearly all the mud frozen up; it was nice for a change. In the evening we went into a cottage close to our farm where there is a family living (only a mile from the firing line) and had a sort of sing song, the French sung one and then we'd sing one. It was rather a weird mixture, carols and 'Tipperary' being mixed together. On the whole I had a jolly good Christmas and I hope you all enjoyed yours as much. I thought of you all often enough and wished I could have been home to hide 'Goodies'. I had more home letters than I can hope to answer individually but may my very best love and thanks go to those who as much touched the parcels and letters. Princess Mary's 'goodie' was also dished out, consisting of not a bad pipe and a not bad box containing cigarettes and baccy. I am using the pipe but shall send the box back if possible.
(*Edward Packe*)

26th December

A day very similar to yesterday, but thaw started in afternoon. Truce still continued – no firing of any description. Spent the day strengthening defences and Field General Court Martial today on Privates Pope and Carter.

27th December

Truce still continued. Much rain today. Owing to the shortage of officers in the battalion (11 including Quarter Master) 5 officers have been lent to us by London Rifle Brigade from today.

28th December

The Battalion was ordered to evacuate Touquet-Berthe farm which had been occupied by the reserve company to the right trench and it was handed over to the Hants. The Dressing Station was also moved to a farm south of Regent Street at a point about 200 yards from where it joins the Messines-Ploegsteert road. The truce continued today but about 8.00 p.m. the Germans sent over to say they were going to continue firing at midnight. However no shots were fired in our vicinity. A very wild night. Gale from SW and much rain.

> Relieved 'C' Company in front line yesterday evening. There is no firing on our front! What a change has come over it! It seems that during the last few days our men and the enemy have been fraternizing and exchanging souvenirs. Today our men and Germans are walking about together in 'No man's Land,' joking and laughing with each other and shaking hands vigorously. You had to see it to believe your eyes! After exchanging cigars for cigarettes they would stroll about arm in arm! I too went out and had a chat with several Germans, most of whom spoke good English. They all looked extremely well and assured us they would not shoot as long as we didn't, so I don't know who will start the ball rolling again here. We are making the most of this fantastic situation while it lasts, for it enables us to bring in our dead who have been lying about since December 19 and give them proper burial in the cemetery near Battalion Headquarters at Somerset House in Ploegsteert Wood. The Germans themselves handed over the body of Captain Maud and told us he was a very brave man.
> (*Arthur Cook*)

29th December

After very bad night it turned out a very fine day. Truce still continued opportunity was taken of it to strengthen the defences considerably. Field General Court Martial for trial of Privates Smith, Allen and Sloman.

> Two surprise shells of ours go over, the first since Christmas Eve, there was still a truce as regards firing in the trenches and it was queer to walk about on the top and see the Germans doing the same. Weather clears up. Spend night on a biscuit box keeping our fire in the trench going. A fire in the trench was only possible because of the truce.
> (*Edward Packe*)

30th December

Frosty night. Brilliantly fine day. Truce still continues. A draft of 8 officers and 86 men arrived unexpectedly last night.

Good progress made today with breastworks behind right trench; also supporting breastworks. The Germans sent the following message to the left trench this morning.

'Dear Camerades,
I beg to inform you that it is forbidden us to go over to you, but we will remain good camerades. If we shall be forced to fire we will fire to high. Please tell me if you are English or Irishmen. Offering you some cigars, I remain yours truly camerade
X.Y'

No answer was given to this communication.

31st December

After a fine night there was much rain today. Some progress was made with the new supporting breastwork. Boyd Fort was also commenced in earnest today. The wiring in front of the new breastwork was practically completed. The G.O.C. 11th Brigade visited the trenches tonight. He did not reach our right trench until about midnight. The Germans celebrated New Year with great vigour. Trumpets were sounded and other instruments played and there was much singing. They also had lanterns hung on the wire entanglements. At 11.00 p.m. they fired a feu de joie over our heads. This was taken by our guns to mean an intended attack and they started shelling. The G.O.C. arrived as the New Year came in and visited our trenches and the houses and farms to the left of the trench, making a very careful inspection in each and all and making many suggestions for improvements.

In the evening moved down to the Piggeries. Have food with some of the London Rifle Brigade.
THE TRUCE IS OVER AND THE WAR STARTS AGAIN.
(*Edward Packe*)

Epilogue

Well over one thousand men of the 1st Battalion, Somerset Light Infantry crossed to France on 22nd August 1914. (It is thought that the 1st Reserve embarked with the Regular Battalion.) Four days later they had lost a quarter of their strength at the battle of Ligny (Le Cateau), including 63 killed or missing and 180, mainly wounded, prisoners of war.

During the next four months there was a general attrition in men, another 100 or so died, many more returning to England wounded, sick or unfit. At the end of December 266 of the original contingent remained with the Battalion. Of course they were partially replaced by recalled reservists, the Special Reserve, and later on in 1915 by the first of the volunteers of August 1914. But the regular soldiers were now in the minority and it was up to the new men to carry on the fight.

The Somersets remained in France and Flanders for the whole of the War and took part in all the major campaigns. The losses continued during 1915, particularly during the Second battle of Ypres where another 26 'Old Contempibles' were killed at St. Julien and Frenzenberg. The Battalion then moved to the Somme and after spending winter in the trenches went into training for 'The Big Push'. On 1st July they were part of the 11th Brigade attack on the Redan Ridge. Here they suffered extremely heavy casualties including 151 killed of which 31 were members of the first contingent.

The Battalion then made a brief return to the Ypres Salient where another 15 perished during a German poison gas attack.

From then on to the end of hostilities the Somersets were involved in most of the major actions but the 'Old Contemptibles' were only a tiny fraction of the Battalion and so the recorded deaths are competitively small, totalling only 17.

At the Armistice only a handful of men had served continuously with the 1st Somersets from 4th August 1914 to 11th November 1918. Of these most were demobilised early in 1919 but a few continued to serve in the Regiment into the 1920's.

Figure 22
Officers Graves, Ploegstreet Wood. (*Somerset Light Infantry Archive*)

Notes

1. There are no specific casualty figures for the Battalion and so it is not possible to compile accurate lists, so all figures quoted above can only be estimates. However, approximate totals gleaned from the 1914 Star Medal Rolls and the Soldiers who Died records show that during the course of the War from the First Contingent, 264 died, 180 were discharged through wounds or sickness, 182 taken Prisoner of War and 224 transferred to other units.

2. The December 1914 Casualty Return from 11th Infantry Brigade War Diary is shown in Appendix 4. This however only reflects the position that the Commanding Officer was aware of at the time.

Appendix One

Sources

The table shows the names of officers and men referred to in the book together with the mains sources from which the information was obtained. Brief details of service are shown where possible.

Bailey *Corporal*	Enlisted 1909	Newspaper Article, Chard and Ilminster News, Chard
Bradshaw, F S *Lieutenant*	Joined Regiment 1904 Killed in Action 19th December 1914	Typescript Diary, Liddle Collection, University of Leeds Library
Cook, Arthur *Private*	Enlisted 1910 Continued service after War Chief Warder, Tower of London Distinguished Conduct Medal Military Medal	1.Original Manuscript Diary Somerset Light Infantry Archive 2. Published as 'A Soldiers War' edited by G Molesworth, Goodman, Taunton, 1957
Dennys, K *Lieutenant*	Prisoner of War 19th December 1914	Committee on Treatment of Prisoners of War, National Archive, WO 161 99-100
Evans *Private*		Newspaper Article, Bath Chronicle, Somerset Study Centre
Fussell, Charles *Private*	Enlisted 1902 Prisoner of War 26th August 1914 Escaped to England 16th October 1916 Military Medal	Typescript Report, Somerset Light Infantry Archive
Green, Arthur *Private*	Wounded and Prisoner War 26th August 1914 Repatriated January 1916	'The Story of a Prisoner of War', Chatto and Windus 1916
Hooper, B *Private*		Newspaper Article, Somerset County Gazette, Taunton

Kelson, Charles *Corporal*	Enlisted 1907 Discharged Wounded 1916	Newspaper Article, Bath Chronicle, Somerset Study Centre
Lewis, T *Private*		Newspaper Article, Somerset County Gazette, Taunton
Miles, Archibald *Bandsman (Stretcher Bearer)*		Newspaper Article, Bath Chronicle, Somerset Study Centre
Nash, E *Private*		Newspaper Article, Somerset County Gazette, Taunton
Packe, Edward *Private*	Enlisted August 1914 Commissioned 1915 Transferred to Royal Flying Corp Served with RAF 2nd World War	Typescript Diary and Correspondence, Liddle Collection, University of Leeds Library
Parkman, Thomas *Private*	Enlisted 1903 Discharged Sick 1915	Newspaper Article, Wells Journal, Somerset Study Centre
Parr, George Rowarth *Lieutenant*	Joined Regiment 1912 Killed in Action 19th December 1914	Published Correspondence
Philby, O C C *Lieutenant*	Wounded and Prisoner of War 26th August 1914 Repatriated December 1918	Typescript Diary, Somerset Light Infantry Archive
Prideaux, G *Lieutenant*	Killed in Action 19th January 1917	1.Original Manuscript Diary Somerset Light Infantry Archive 2. Published as 'A Soldiers Diary', Privately, 1918
Tadd, J. *Lance Corporal*	Discharged August 1915	Newspaper Article, Bath Chronicle, Somerset Study Centre
Thwaites, N G *Lieutenant Colnel*	4th Dragoon Guards	'A Walk around Plug Street' Tony Spangoly and Ted Smith, Leo Cooper 1997
Watson, William *Captain*	Joined Regiment 1900 Killed in Action 3rd May 1917	Typescript Diary Somerset Light Infantry Archive
Wevell, Thomas *Private*	Enlisted 1897 Died of Wounds 1st October 1914	Newspaper Article, Bath Chronicle, Somerset Study Centre
Whittuck, G E M *Lieutenant*		Typescript Diary Somerset Light Infantry Archive
Wyrrell, E		History of the Somerset Light Infantry 1914–1919 Reprinted 2002 Naval and Military Press

Appendix Two

Bibliography of books relating to the Somerset Light Infantry

18 Platoon by Sidney Jary, Private Publication, 1987. (Refers to 4th Battalion, Europe 1944–1945.)

4th Battalion Somerset Light Infantry by C G Lipscombe, Private Publication. (Refers to Europe 1944–1945.)

Answering the Call by John H F Mackie. Raby, 2002. (Refers to the 2/4th Battalion 1914–1919.)

Book of Remembrance 5th Battalion by Major E S Goodland and Captain H L Milsom, Private, Chiswick Press, 1930. Republished Naval and Military Press, 2003. (Refers to 1/5th and 2/5th Battalions 1914–1919.)

Correspondence of George Rowarth Parr, Private Circulation. (Refers to the 1st Battalion 1914.)

Door Marked Malaya by Oliver Crawford, Rupert Hart-Davis Ltd 1958. (Refers to Somerset Light Infantry in Malay, 1950s.)

Engaged in War by Stanley Goodland, Twiga Books, 1999. (Refers to the 1/5th and 2/5th Battalions 1914–1919.)

Forged by Fire by Brendon Moorhouse, Spellmont, 2003. (Refers to the 7th Battalion 1914–1919.)

Fromes Fallen Heroes by David Adams, 2000. (References to Somerset Light Infantry men 1914–1919.)

Historical Record of the Thirteenth, First Somerset, or the Prince Albert's Regiment of Light Infantry by Richard Canon, Parker, Furnival and Parker, 1848.

Historical Record of the Thirteenth, First Somersetshire, or Prince Albert's Regiment of Light Infantry by Thomas Carter, W O Mitchell, 1867.

History of 1st Battalion, The Somerset Light Infantry (Prince Albert's). July 1st 1916 to the end of the War by Major V H B Majendie, D.S.O. Goodman, 1921.

History of the Somerset Light Infantry (Prince Albert's): 1685–1914 by Sir Henry Everett.

History of the Somerset Light Infantry (Prince Albert's): 1946-1960 by Kenneth Whitehead. Somerset Light Infantry, 1961, Republished Naval and Military Press, 2004.

No Thankful Village: The Impact of the Great War on a Group of Somerset Villages by Chris Howell, Fickle Hill, 2002. (Makes references to Somerset Light Infantry men 1914–1919.)

Scrapbook of the 7th Battalion, Somerset Light Infantry (13th Foot) by Captain J L Meredith, Frederick Samuel, 1932 (Refers to the 7th Battalion 1914–1919.)

Short History of the Somerset Light Infantry, Cale and Polden, 1929

Soldiers Diary of the Great War by Captain GA Prideaux M.C. Private Circulation, 1918 (refers to the 1st Battalion 1914–1917.)

Soldiers Died in the Great War 1914–19: Prince Albert's (Somerset Light Infantry), H.M.S.O., 1921

Soldiers War by Arthur Henry Cook, Goodman and Sons, 1957 (Refers to the 1st Battalion 1914–19.)

Somerset Light Infantry (Prince Albert's)(the 13th Regiment of Foot) by Hugh Popham, Hamish Hamilton, 1968.

Somerset Light Infantry 1685–1968: Records of Honour by Liz Grant, Somerset Books, 2004.

Somerset Light Infantry 1914–9 by Everard Wyrell, Methuan, 1927. Republished Naval and Military Press, 2002.

Story of a Prisoner of War by Arthur Green, Chatto and Windus 1916. (Refers to the 1st Battalion 1914, Prisoner of War 1914–15.)

Strange War by C P Mills. Allan Sutton, 1988 (Refers to the 2/5th Battalion 1914–1919.)

Appendix Three

War establishment of infantry units

Field Service Pocket Book, 1914

9.—HEADQUARTERS OF A DIVISION.

Commander.

Lieutenant or Major-General.

Personal Appointments.

2 Aides-de-camp.

Staff.

1 General staff officer, 1st grade.
1 ,, ,, ,, 2nd ,,
1 ,, ,, ,, 3rd ,,
1 Asst. adjt. and quartermaster-general.
1 Dep. asst. adjt. and quartermaster-general.
1 Dept. asst. quartermaster-general.

Administrative Services.

1 Asst. director of medical services.
1 Dep. asst. dir. of medical services.
1 Asst. director of veterinary services.
1 Dep. asst. director of ordnance services.
— Army postal service (3 clerks).

Special Appointment.

1 Asst. provost-marshal.

Police, clerks, &c.

Note.—(1) When a division is acting independently, 1 G.S.O., 3rd grade, with 3 horses and 2 batmen will be added.
(2) The asst. director medical services commands the R.A.M.C. of the division.

10.—AN INFANTRY BRIGADE.*
(After Concentration.)

Detail.	Personnel.		Horses.				Machine Guns.	Vehicles.				Bicycles.
								Carts.		Wagons.		
	Officers.	Other Ranks.	Riding.	Draught.	Heavy Draught.	Pack.		1-horsed.	2-horsed.	2-horsed.	4-horsed.	
Headquarters ...	4	23	13	8	2	...	...	...	1	...	2	...
4 Battalions ...	120	3,908	52	104	32	36	8	4	32	28	...	36
	124	3,931	65	112	34	36	8	4	33	28	2	36

11.—HEADQUARTERS OF AN INFANTRY BRIGADE.

Commander.

Brigadier-general.

Staff.

1 Brigade-major.
1 Staff captain.

Administrative Services

1 Veterinary officer.
— Army postal service (3 clerks).

Police, clerks, &c.

12.—WAR ESTABLISHMENT OF VARIOUS UNITS—*continued*.
(Including attached but excluding details left at base.) For details of transport *see* p. 120.

| Unit. | Personnel. | | Horses. | | | | Guns. | | Vehicles (excluding gun carriages and limbers). | | | | | | | |
| | | | | | | | | | Carts. | | Wagons. | | | | | |
	Officers.	Other ranks.	Riding.	Draught.	Heavy draught.	Pack.	Guns.	Machine guns.	1-horsed.	2-horsed.	2-horsed.	4-horsed.	6-horsed.	Motor cars.	Bicycles.	Motor cycles.
Infantry :—																
Battalion..	30	977	13	26	8	9	..	2	1	12‡	3	..	..	..	9	..
Hdqrs. and M.G. Section	6	93	9	26	..	1	..	2	1	8	3	..	..	..	9	..
Company..	6	221	1	..	2	2	..	..	..	1‡	..	..	..	..	..	..

* Includes lorries, &c.   † Lorries.   ‡ Includes travelling kitchens.

Appendix Four

1st Battalion, Somerset Light Infantry Return of Casualties, December 1914*

1. Numbers who came out with the Battalion on 22.8.14 and have served continuously since.

       5   Officers   266   Other ranks

2. Total casualties to date.

	Officers	
Killed	8.	Major F.G.Thoyts, Captains C.C.Maud, F.S. Bradshaw, R.C. Orr. Lieutenants R.L. Moore, G.R.Parr. 2nd Lieutenants A.B.Read, S.B.Henson
Wounded	12.	Major C.W. Compton, Captains L.A. Jones Mortimer, J. M. Smith, N. A. H. Campbell, G. E. M. Whittuck, Lieutenants A. V. Newton, R. J. R. Leacroft, R. V. Montgomery, J .W. M. Vincent, 2nd Lieutenants J. S. Bush, E. E. Glossop, R. A. A. Chichester
Wounded & Missing	6	Captains A. J. G. Hargreaves, J. G. N. Broderip, Lieutenants J. B. Taylor, O. G. B. Philby, J. C. W. Macbryan, 2nd Lieutenant K. G. G. Dennys
Missing	1	Captain C. K. Holden R.A.M.C.
Hospital	10	Lieutenant Colonels E.H. Swayne, C.B. Prowse, Captain W. Watson, Lieutenants E. P. Pretyman, C. T. Holt, K. J. Miller, G. A. Prideaux, R. A. B. Watts, 2nd Lieutenant V. A. Braithwaite
TOTAL	37	

---

* Source; WO95/1486 Public Records Office

Other ranks

Killed	131
Wounded	434
Wounded/ Missing	58
Missing	80
Hospital	450
TOTAL	1135

3. Numbers who came out with the Battalion and have rejoined after sickness or absence due to wounds

      Officers

3	Major C.W Compton
	Captain F.S Bradshaw (Since Killed)
	Lieutenant G.R Parr (Since Killed)

      Other Ranks

25	C. W. Compton, Major, commanding 1/Somerset Light Infantry 28/12/1914